SARA

MINDY BLUMENFELD

THERAPY, SHMERAPY

DEMYSTIFYING THERAPY
Even for People Who Don't Need It

Copyright © **2017 Hamodia Treasures**

ISBN: **9781-60091-514-790000**

All rights reserved
No part of this publication may be translated,
reproduced, stored in a retrieval system or transmitted, in any form or by any means,
electronic, mechanical, photocopying, recording, or otherwise, without prior written
permission from the publisher.

Published by: **Hamodia Treasures**
207 Foster Avenue, Brooklyn, NY 11230
Book design and layout: **Shoshana Radunsky**
Distributed by: **Israel Book Shop**
501 Prospect Street #97, Lakewood, New Jersey 08701
Telephone 732-901-3009 Fax 732-901-4012
www.israelbookshoppublications.com

Printed in Canada

Dedication

To three mentors, *mentschen,* good-enough mothers
KCT MSEd, LCSW
Mary Ann Cappellino, LCSW
Elizabeth Janssen MA, NP, PMHCNS, BC

In this book is all you have taught me.
It is the story of a thousand tales that began with you.

And to my mother,
Chedva Weinberger. No initials needed
My childhood was exactly what I needed.
It — and *you* — was as close to perfect as it could have possibly been.

Acknowledgments

When my oldest son married, I remember sending out invitations to the most seemingly random people. To Chayie, who played backgammon with me in the bungalow colony when I was seven years old, and she was seventeen. To friends I had not spoken to in years. To my counselor in camp; the family that welcomed me into their home when I spent my seminary year in Israel; and family friends I had lost touch with more than two decades earlier.

Within each invitation, I wrote a thank-you letter to each of these individuals who had touched me in ways that allowed me to grow as a person and a mother. I wanted them each to know that their random acts of kindness and caring had been part of the person I had become, capable of raising this special son, who in turn was marrying a girl with sterling qualities. For the seed I had been, filled with potential but needing soil, sunlight, and water to blossom, each of these people had been that nurturing environment for me. And Chayie flew in from Florida for the wedding, acknowledging the truth of how it takes a village to raise a child.

And now, as this book comes to fruition, I want to thank all those people who knowingly or unknowingly helped give birth to this book — my sixth child, if you will.

Mrs. Shirley Sokol, my second grade teacher, who taught me even then that if I could read, if I acquired an education, there was nothing I could not do. And to my high school teachers, Mrs. Faige Wolpin, a distinguished *mechaneches* and *kallah* teacher; Mrs. Briendy Koppelman, *menaheles* of Bais Yaakov Machon Chen of Switzerland; and Rebbetzin Landau, *a"h*, a *Chumash* teacher beyond compare. You all believed in me during my crazy high school days, and for that I thank you.

To Mrs. Nomi Weiss, now of Bnos Sarah Seminary (where my daughter spent the most wonderful seminary year), who provided a home away from home when I was in seminary twenty years earlier. Her example as mother, wife, and exemplary human being has guided me as a therapist as well.

I thank with all my heart Rebbetzin Bruria David, *menaheles* of BJJ, for having the vision to create a place for incredible development. Your most powerful lesson is how we must view ourselves as growth-oriented individuals without hiding behind our roles of mother, daughter, wife. Our lives must have meaning irrespective of these roles, and I try to impart that philosophy to my clients who may not be mothers, daughters, or wives and yet their lives are imbued with meaning — if they can just find it.

To my childhood friends, whose creativity, love of reading, writing, and imagination was fertile ground for my adult passion to read and write and create. For those gilded summer Morningside Acre days, I thank you: Chayie (Feder) Goldring; Rivki (Freund) Jungreis; Miriam (Freund) Ungar; Esti (Fettman) Spitzer; Ruchie (Feder) Gross; Raiza (Schonbrun) Silber; Chany (Kauftheil) Schwartz; and to all your mothers who treated me like family. I will never forget the hikes we took in which we seamlessly integrated the outdoors with discussions about the classics and the meaning of life. Hard to believe that we were only ten years old then…

When I need creative and productive outlets, I could not survive without my Scrabble group. Thank you, Rivka Blima Klein, Toby Klein, Zeesy Gruen, and Mindy Steinmetz. I forgive you all for never letting me win.

For enriching my life in ways beyond the time we actually spend together, what would I have done without my Writing Group? Thank you, Ricky Bronner, Gitty Epstein, Adina Katz, Malky Mitnik, Esther Perr, Miriam Rusi Perr, Rivky Posner, Sarah Rothstein, Mimi Weinfeld, Pia Wolcowitz, and of course, the incredible Faygie Borchadt, who leads us to

ACKNOWLEDGMENTS

writing triumph. We do good therapy each time we meet!

To my wonderful sister group, Ruchie Kauftheil, Esti Stauber, and Raizy Gornish. I am so grateful we are family, because I can't imagine you would have put up with me under any other circumstances. We know how to have fun! (And none of you need therapy...)

To the Blumenfeld family, my sisters-in-law, my mother-in-law, and everyone else who had no idea what and why I was doing what I did, but accepted and loved me anyway.

To all my terrific clients (you know who you are), thank you so much for all you have taught me. For your courage to allow me in your journey of healing, for letting me know when I botched up, for forgiving me and trusting me anyway. For all the boundaries we have to keep, my admiration and respect to you all is boundary-less!

For the support of my peers and colleagues, breaking the alienation of our solitary work, I am privileged to be in my various supervision groups. To my brilliant EMDR colleagues, thank you, Linda Chabbot, Chaya Friedman, Alexander Rand, Ari Roth, and Toby Werdyger. We survived though our supervisors may have not. Nobody can accuse this group of a lack of personality.

I am grateful to have been part of Ricki Bernstein's incredible somatic intervention training and joining her in supervision.

My newly formed, dynamic peer supervision group, I am so excited to begin our journey together. Thank you, Chaya Sarah Brevda-Ghoori, Esther Goldstein-Lindner, Joseph Lovecchio, Yaakov Schiff, Ari Sorotzkin, and Shulamis (Gitel) Weber.

Thank you, Dr. Nancy Gallina, Assistant Dean of Touro College School of Social Work. Your support, supervision, mentoring, and belief in me means the world to me. I could have never done it without you. You are a role model of social work, of altruism, of what it means to make a difference.

A heartfelt thank you to a valiant and courageous warrior who faces life challenges with the same sense of humor with which she suggested to me the title of this book. Thank you Judith Guedalia, PhD Dir. Neuropsychology Unit of Shaare Zedek Medical Center in Jerusalem; Co-Chair and Founder of Nefesh Israel. Thank you all of the listserv of Nefesh International for your continuous opportunities to learn, obtain support, and to simply be entertained.

To my dearest parents, Mr. and Mrs. Pinchus and Chedva Weinberger, there are no words to thank parents who raised me with strong values, a commitment to family, and a strong foundation of self. Thank you for believing in me, loving me, and supporting me. And thank you for not giving me up for adoption when I was a teenager. I really appreciate it!

To my special children, my greatest gifts, my reason to celebrate life in all its glory and glamour. I won't mention that when I began my first semester in social work school, my oldest, then leaving to Eretz Yisrael for his first *zman* in Yeshivas Kaminetz, said, "Ma, all social workers' kids are nuts. I am leaving just in time!"

I won't even talk about how my daughter said, "The years you were in school were the worst years of my life."

Nor will I write how my fourth complained that I did not pop popcorn for snack each morning as I had done for the past years, or that he was condemned to store-bought *challos* because of college.

And I will certainly omit my youngest child's tragic summing up of his childhood: "I grew up without a mother."

So a kiss to all my brave and suffering children and their spouses, Kasriel and Suri Blumenfeld; Refael Ahron and Racheli Schonberger; Moshe Dov and Hindy Blumenfeld; Tzvi David, and Hillel. I adore you and all the grandchildren to pieces! Thank you for letting me experiment all my therapy techniques on you first. You turned out great!

And finally, to the one person who has been on this journey with me from when we first met in my parents' home 28 years ago, sitting at the glass table in the dining room, too excited and nervous to breathe, not knowing that our marriage would be the most wonderful experience that would ever happen to us. To my dear husband, Yitzchok Blumenfeld,

ACKNOWLEDGMENTS

you have not only given me the wings to fly, but you have been the wind beneath my wings, the cloud to carry me when my wings drooped, and the mountain upon which I rested. I do not know how to thank you for all you have been and for all you still do. Thank you. Thank you. Thank you.

I thank Hakadosh Baruch Hu for the talents he has bestowed upon me and for guiding me along the way. When I look back at the road less traveled by, He has made all the difference… Of all the roles I have been fortunate to play these many years of wife, mother, grandmother, sister, friend, writer, and therapist, the one identity that supersedes them all is that of being a religious Jew. It all begins and ends with Him, and I would have it no other way.

When You Called Me

Therapy is a gift. A gift to the client, who can unwrap it and find the very best of herself inside; the self that can emerge and give to others. It is a gift to the therapist, who watches the discovery and feels blessed to be a part of this wonder.

As a therapist, I often conceptualize my work as helping clients move through the five levels of Abraham Maslow's *Hierarchy of Needs*. Maslow was a psychologist, and his theory centered around the necessity of fulfilling innate human needs to effect psychological health that will allow a person to reach his fullest potential. These five levels of need, according to Maslow, are what motivate humans to achieve; each level that is achieved leads the person to a higher level of existence.

This hierarchy is depicted as a pyramid. Imagine the wide base of the pyramid, firmly planted on the ground. Then imagine the pyramid rising, narrowing, narrowing, until it reaches a point somewhere high up. Its point perhaps even reaching the sky.

These are the five floors of the pyramid. Our physiological needs. The need for safety. The need for love and belonging. The need to experience self-esteem. And lastly, at the very top, standing on the foundation of the others, is the need for self-actualization.

As a therapist, I attend to each of these needs in order to motivate the client to higher and higher levels of functioning. The essays in this book are grouped around aspects of these needs through the therapeutic lens. I invite you to explore your deepest self through the work in which my clients and I engage, in the words of my clients (who have given me permission to share their beautifully poetic words) and my many supervisors who have guided me — and continue to guide me along this marvelous journey of self-discovery and healing.

The Binah Bunch

In third grade, I wrote my first novel. An action-packed adventure story about three slaves who escape from their Roman masters, set in Ancient times. I threw it away one day when I had brought it to school, showed it to my teacher, and she laughed. I still remember the garbage can on the corner of the block of the school building where I simply dropped a year's worth of writing.

It's very possible, had *Binah* been in existence way back then, you would be holding that novel instead of this book in your hands today. But I needed to wait four more decades to meet the most incredible bunch at *Binah* for that to happen.

I want to thank Ruth Lichtenstein, Editor-in-Chief and Publisher at *Hamodia* and *Binah Magazine*; a visionary woman who created both a newspaper and magazine of which I am proud to be a part. I admire strong and brilliant women!

There are many people (aren't there always?) to whom I owe a debt of thanks, and my whole-hearted admiration for their expertise, knowledge, and dedication that created this book.

Thank you, Rivky Posner, Chief Operating Officer of *Binah Magazine*, my best friend from high school! To have our paths cross through *Binah* and our writing group has been one of the best things about writing for *Binah*. You hooked me on publishing from that day over thirty years ago, when you showed me the galleys of a book your uncle, Rabbi Abraham Twerski wrote; *Generation to Generation*. How it thrilled me then; how this venture we are on together thrills me now!

Thank you, Rochel Roth, managing editor, whom I first met in her dining room, where I was treated to a scrumptious breakfast as we hashed out the birth of my therapy column, "Therapy: a sneak peek inside," which became the basis of this book.

To the other members of both the *Binah* staff and my writing group, Faygie Borchadt, editorial consultant; and Esther Perr, coordinating editor; thank you for you insight, ideas and support. To know you both personally and professionally has been my honor (and fun!).

Suri Koplowitz, associate editor — your emails clog up my inbox (alongside the fan mail for "Therapy: a sneak peek inside") and you are always right! That's why I never argue with you. And we figure out good titles together...

Sara Bonchek, copy editor; I love the job you do, and the little notes you send me on the margins all over my columns. You miss nothing and I appreciate being in such capable hands. When people compliment me by commenting on how every sentence in my column packs a punch, it's your editing they are referring to.

Thank you, Toby Morgenstern, production manager, for your timely reminders that my columns and articles are due even when I am untimely, time and time again! Your patience and perseverance are praiseworthy.

Shiffy Rosenberg, technical coordinator; my thanks to you for all the times you went out of your way to do those annoying favors for me, like checking up the word count when I could not access my documents, and making it seem like it was no big deal.

Chaya Paneth, editorial support, for making sure everything gets where it needs to be (which she is very good at).

I am privileged to work with Chavi Ernster, manager of *Hamodia Treasures*, whose first correspondence with me was of a philosophical nature. Now that we both know who we are, thank you for your two cents worth, which is worth millions to me in this production of my book.

Thank you, Shoshana Rudansky, graphic designer of my book cover and overall layout, for your magnificent work. Artistic talent always takes my breath away.

Rachel Hubner, editor and go-to girl at *Hamodia*, thank you for that final (and all) review of my book to catch all the stuff everyone else missed.

To someone I trust implicitly, Rebbetzin Leah Kohn, content director; thank you so much for your insight and suggestions. There is something very special in knowing that any piece of writing I publish meets the highest standards.

To an exceptional person at *Hamodia*, who although she is not involved specifically in the production of this book, has been the driving force of all my writing from when I first sat in her Language Arts class in the tenth grade of Bais Yaakov High School.

Tobi Einhorn, senior editor; when you first assigned those writing journals and fired us up with the power of the written word through your literature lessons, you created a storm in me. I simply had to write. I wrote and wrote all that year, and when you handed me back my journals with an A++, you also created a writer. Your love of your students, your chosen career, and your own modeled writing were what enabled me to write even when all my teachers, from third grade through twelfth, thought my efforts were mediocre and lacking talent, and slashed up my compositions and essays with red pens identifying every single grammar mistake and inconsistent verb tense.

Because of you, I wrote anyway.

I am so glad I did.

So thank you, Tobi Einhorn. I am only one of thousands of students you have impacted.

> Mindy Blumenfeld has a most captivating way of connecting. Although a thorough, absolute professional in all her dealings, within this book, we connect with her as if with our next door neighbor, or our sister's best friend. This very serious material is shared with humor and warmth. We see that this 'therapy' business does make perfectly good sense.
>
> *- Miriam Liebermann, MSW*
> Co-author of Saying Goodbye, *a guidebook for those dealing with grief and bereavement and author of* The Best is Yet to Be *and* To Fill the Sky with Stars, *anthologies for women in the transitional years.*

> The world of mental illness and its recovery often seems incomprehensible and shrouded in mystery. In her collection of columns and articles, Mindy Blumenfeld guides the reader though the labyrinth of Borderline Personality Disorders, "transference" and numerous other seemingly arcane aspects of this field in a colloquial, coherent and unpretentious fashion. It's a must read for those who want to "tour" the world of a psychotherapist.
>
> ***-Dr. Norman Blumenthal***
>
> *Zachter Family Chair in Trauma and Crisis Counseling*
> *Director, OHEL Miriam Center for Trauma, Bereavement and Crisis Response*
>
> *Educational Director & Adjunct Professor*
> *Bella and Harry Wexner Kollel Elyon & Semikha Honors Program*
> *Yeshiva University*
>
> *Assistant Professor, Hofstra Northwell School of Medicine*
> *Faculty Lead, Group Therapy Training Program*

> I am impressed by Mindy's keen insights on psychotherapy. There is still much misunderstanding about therapy, especially in the *frum* world, and *Therapy, Shmerapy* may clarify some of the problems.
>
> *- **Rabbi Abraham J. Twerski, MD***
> *Gateway Rehabilitation Center*
> *Founder, Medical Director Emeritus*

TABLE OF CONTENTS

Part I
The Therapist 25

The New Client 27
Who Needs Therapy, Anyway? 31
What I Want to Be When I Grow Up 34
Who's Who in Therapy 37
When Talk Is Cheap, Is It Worth It? 41
Who Am I? Ethics in the Therapy Room 45
Yes, Even Therapists Need Therapists! 48
Bloopers: Mistakes I Have Made as a Therapist 52

Part II
The Client 57

Defense Mechanisms 59
Enigma of Stigma 62
Selfish in Therapy 66
Mandate Reporting 69
Our Community Does Not Recognize Evil 72
Protecting Those Who Once Protected Us 76
The Borderline Mother 80
The Borderline Mother Revisited: A Therapist Apologizes ... 84
Deprived Of Touch, We Lose Our Touch 88

Part III
The Therapist and Client 93

Bound to Have Boundaries 95
Following Up On "Bound to Have Boundaries" 99
Hoopla About the Hug 109
Therapist, What Do You See When I Sit in Your Office? ... 113
Therapy Is Not Helping, Part 1 117
Therapy Is Not Helping Me, Part 2 121
If I'm Paying for Therapy, I Must See Results! 125
Therapist Love 129

Part IV
The Family **133**

A Therapist Speaks to the Parents of Her Client............................ 134
A Therapist Speaks to the Parents of her Client, Part 2 138
Glue, Tape, and Documents: Not the Only Attachments 142
When Friends Fly, and Clients Cry 146
Acts of Betrayal: She Might Not Know, But the Relationship Will! 149
Shidduchim and Therapy Secrets 152
A Note to Our Sponsors (of Spirituality) 156
A Coupla Stuff About Couples 160
Family Fun Time: When Therapy Can Flummox the Family 164

Part V
The Therapy.. **169**

Going Public on Private Practice 171
Therapus Terminexus: Why Didn't You Say So? 174
Controversy About Consent: When Parents Don't Know................178
Just a Spoonful of Medicine Makes the Down Go Down... 182
Form. Storm. Perform. 186
EMDR 190
Sandtray Therapy..194
The One I Don't Speak About...198
Living With a Therapist 203

Goodbye — A Client Terminates **207**
GLOSSARY **209**
About the Author **213**

Part I
The Therapist

Air. Water. Food. Clothing. Shelter.

The base of the pyramid of Maslow's hierarchy of needs is the widest, the one that takes up the most space in our lives, yet it is the most primitive. It is the physiological needs of a person that are centered around survival. If a person lacks those, he cannot concentrate on anything else in his life. When a client comes in suffering panic attacks, there is little we can do by way of improving his life until he knows he can breathe again without fear. If my client is hungry or thirsty, or has no shelter from wind or cold or heat, there can be no dialogue about how to speak without yelling at her children. Her most basic needs of survival must first be addressed.

My clients speak in metaphors, sometimes describing therapy as their most basic survival need.

My client says, "I am a sponge.
And therapy is water. Where I am not, therapy is.
When I am not actively engaged in life,
the water of therapy comes rushing in and floods my every crevice."

My clients says, "Your office is like a warm bath
in which I splash around.
But I wonder if when I leave,
the waters close over the spot where I had once been
and I am forgotten."

Another client evokes the image of food, a basic need, speaking directly to me about our work together:

Therapy, Shmerapy

"You know how when you work with pastry dough,
and you want the filling to stay inside,
you use water to close the ragged edges smoothly?
That is how I think of what you [therapist] have done.
Worked with me until the dough smoothed over,
closing the gaps and wounds.
I thank you for what you have given me;
your words."

PART I THE THERAPIST

The New Client

You called me about a week ago.

Maybe you read my column; maybe you heard me speak somewhere. Maybe someone mentioned my name.

And the things you have been thinking about for the past few days, even the past few years, suddenly seem to loom over you like a black cloud, fogging your sight, not letting you breathe. It was easy to find my number. Maybe you sent me an email because that was even easier. It didn't seem as real.

But you called. You contacted me. And I didn't sound so bad over the phone. Not that you knew what to expect. You never went to therapy before. Who, you? Nobody would even dream you needed therapy. Successful in school/yeshivah, great at your job, model parent, seemingly happy and social and has it all.

Or maybe, you had gone to therapy. Years ago. Some lady at school. Boy, was that weird. You hated it. Some guy in this office your father dragged you to because he said he needed to make a *mentsch* out of you. And the guy was not bad. You played with cars. Or cards. Or some video game. And you weren't sure what exactly you were doing there. You are not exactly sure even now why you called. Or what you want. But you know something's not right. And you wonder if maybe therapy will help.

So you wake up with a pit in your stomach one Monday a week after you have called me. You have an appointment with me. And you are also feeling butterflies. Maybe even plain caterpillars crawling inside of you. A little nervous, a little excited. A little resigned, a little hopeful. You wonder what

I look like and what the session will be like. You wonder how on earth I can even help you. Especially when all your life you have been the one helping everyone else.

And I wonder, too.

When I take out a new manila folder, and put a fresh new paper inside of it and an Agreement for Treatment inside of it, I get a nervous, excited feeling too.

I will be opening a brand new book, plunging into the first chapter.

Then you ring the bell, and as I walk outside my office to the front door of my floor, I wonder who I will see.

I smile at you (because I am happy to see you, curious about this new adventure), and welcome you in.

I imagine my office from behind your eyes and wonder what you see. (Sometimes, I know, you see nothing at all, the room a hazy cloud, me a cloudy figure with blurred facial features.)

A blue couch on your right, two leather white armchairs on your left. My sand tray and figurines on the wall opposite. Two clocks ticking relentlessly. Comforting, too. You wonder if I treat children (no, teens and adults only) because I have so many toys and things in my room. A Hoberman sphere (you need to see it to understand it), a slinky, a red blanket, some balls. A puzzle piece, a squishy brain, a large cup of candies and lollipops. Deeper in my room you notice a dollhouse and trucks, and you may wonder what is inside the drawers (arts and crafts materials; clay).

One day, if you hang in long enough, you will ask me why I have all these things. You may ask me why I have a glass jar of shells and rocks from the ocean and beaches. And over time, you will settle into the therapy room, and it will become yours and the toys and rocks and candies will be yours, too. And you will learn the answers on your own, and with my help. (If you read this book, you may find out these answers without the sweat and blood and tears of therapy. And maybe without the joys either, but that is your choice.)

What else do you see when you enter my room?

You see my little library of books. If you care to browse you may learn about me. What I read reveals much of who I am. What interests me. What kind of therapist I am. Who I admire. What I respect. It is only a slice because the greater part of my library resides in my home. But still.

You will also see my diplomas and certificates hanging on the wall.

A calendar.

A collage I once made, the center of which is dominated by a great, roaring tiger. If you stay with me long enough, and notice the abundance of tigers in my room, you may ask me about them. And because I do self-disclose, using it as another tool in therapy, we may talk about these tigers one day. And then perhaps you will tell me about yours as well.

There are pillows in my room. For resting your head. Or for supporting your back. Sometimes, for hugging. There are pashminas. For warmth. For twisting between your fingers. A box of tissues (even two) for nose-blowing and tear-wiping. A weighted blanket for calming, the scent of cinnamon and potpourri soothing.

In the corner of the room opposite the calendar, tucked away so that you cannot see it, but I can, is a painting I made, even though I cannot draw. It is another thing one day we may talk about. I doubt on this first day you notice much.

Because today, you come in hesitant.

Because today, this is an interview, and neither of us want to fail.

How can you help me, you are wondering. And I want to tell you everything. I want to tell you how I am an object relations therapist, one who views all of our problems through the lens of attachment. How as little ones, we attach and are loved, cared for, by our primary caregivers. Our mothers. Our fathers. Or not loved enough.

I want to tell you that although I assess through the lens of attachment, there are many ways I have learned with which to help my clients.

There's talk therapy, of course. But also CBT (cognitive behavioral therapy), somatic work, EMDR, and family or couples counseling. I integrate narrative therapy, mindfulness, sand tray therapy, and use of materials like clay or collage.

Therapy, Shmerapy

If you ask me, "How will therapy help me?" I will answer you. I may explain how trauma impacts a person, if the trauma happened two days ago — or twenty years ago. I will explain about *little t trauma* and *Big T trauma* and how *little t traumas* can be just as traumatic as *Big T* ones. If you ask, if you want to know, I can explain any and all of the different types of therapies and interventions I have listed here.

If you ask me, "How long will I need to be in therapy?" I can answer that, too.

Sometimes the answer will be six weeks, and sometimes the answer will be six months. And even six years. If you are interested, I will explain the reason behind my answer. I can also explain what we will be doing, the plan, and what the therapy journey may look like.

You may not always like my answers, but know I will always be transparent, honest, and real with you. Any good therapist can tell you the same.

Therapy is not some mysterious concoction in which the therapist is a mystical, secretive person who weaves sorcery around a client and results magically appear. I wish.

Although therapy is not an exact science (and there are therapists who may disagree with me), for the most part there is a science to our work, and as therapists we have a responsibility to our clients to be able to identify the problem, formulate a plan to address the problem, and be clear with the client how exactly this plan will be implemented. Including the bumps along the road that may erupt, suddenly strewing pebbles and even rocks into our path, derailing us.

So I ask you, New Client, who is standing in my doorway, hesitating to enter this unknown journey, will you please come in?

There's the couch. There's the chair.

Take your pick.

And I invite you, Reader, to walk inside the pages of this book and follow us in our journey.

It is not for the faint of heart.

But there is room for all of you.

Come.

Take a candy.

PART I THE THERAPIST

Who Needs Therapy, Anyway?

Agoraphobia, Borderline, Conduct Disorder, Depression, Encopresis...

Yep, I know the ABCs of mental disorders pretty well. As a matter of fact, when I sat in Abnormal Psychology classes in college, I thought I had symptoms of every mental disorder we learned about. (While I only *thought* I had them, my kids were absolutely convinced that if their mother was becoming a therapist — gasp! — then she *for sure had them...*).

The good news is that I only have a couple of them, so I am still functional enough to write this column and subsequent ones that will demystify and even detonate (I'm good at that) the mystique of therapy; to render it accessible and understandable to all my readers who suspect that therapy may be helpful to them, or to somebody close to them, but are not sure why or how.

In all seriousness, I remember that not even halfway into my first semester of my graduate program in social work, I sat in one of my classes learning about how to practice therapy, and I was awash with this awe-inspiring feeling of having come home. Home to where I belonged, home to the work that called to me from when I was a small child and felt driven to help every single bug, frog, cat, child, and adult who seemed to be in pain.

And I am utterly grateful to spend my time not only doing the work I love on a daily basis, but to have this opportunity to educate others through this column so that in our community, therapy will be viewed as simply another tool to improve quality of life.

Therapy, Shmerapy

I still remember the days when undergoing speech therapy was a stigma. When a girl in my school could barely speak because of a crippling stutter. When that first grader seemed so cute with her heavy lisp; there were whispers about speech therapy, but nobody dared speak of it aloud.

Today?

Ha. If someone *redts* you a *shidduch* with a girl with a speech impediment, no matter how small or insignificant, immediately judgment is passed and extensive research is done on this apparently neglectful mother who dared not to apply to the Board of Education for speech therapy services.

Undergoing therapy to alleviate emotional distress should be no more of a stigma than undergoing speech or occupational therapy to alleviate problems of a physical nature. In fact, the ramifications of neglecting emotional distress can be even more far reaching than neglecting a physical problem.

Okay, enough with the introduction.

Here's what you really want to know: Why would the average person go to therapy, and how is therapy going to help her?

Loaded, loaded questions.

Very simply, the average person may recognize that she is just not feeling as good as she would like to. This can happen for many reasons, big or small, emotional or physical; and sometimes for no reason at all. She may have tried a bunch of things to get herself together, things that are just not working. She may have tried talking to her husband, her sisters, and friends. She may have tried talking to her Rav, Rebbetzin, or teacher from high school. She may have read *mussar sefarim* and self-help books. She may even have told herself firmly, "Just stop acting/thinking/feeling like this and be normal!" And even though she was really, really strict and self-disciplined, it didn't help.

She may be feeling depressed or anxious. She may be thinking thoughts that don't belong in her head or feelings that don't belong in her heart. She may be acting in ways that hurt others, or hurt herself, either physically or emotionally. She may be unable to do things she normally does easily, or cannot engage in enjoyable activities that she once did, or enjoy things she has never been able to enjoy that she knows others do. She may realize that her relationship with others, or with herself, is stunted, and want more for herself. She may simply know somehow that the life she is living, or has lived until now, is just not what Hashem wants of her; that something is missing, and although she has tried to find that elusive something, she has been unsuccessful.

The truth? Therapy works best for emotionally healthy people.

So how does therapy work?

Loaded, loaded, very loaded question.

There are so many different types of therapies that it is beyond the scope of this article to enumerate and explain them all. Suffice to say that although therapy can never be an exact science — every therapeutic experience is unique, because of the individuality of each person and the individuality of each client-therapist relationship — there is research enough to validate the efficacy of the various types of therapy.

Different forms of therapy are used to target different issues, although the single most important tool used in therapy is the therapist's self, without which few other interventions can take effect.

Change happens through the talking and listening done in therapy; through the specific techniques of individual types of therapies; through the dynamics of the therapeutic alliance developed.

Therapy works. Therapy changes people and their circumstances. And when change happens that illuminates a person's life and gives a person the opportunity to be the individual she wants to be, you want to be there.

So if you want to master your ABCs, stick around and get to know your friendly, neighborhood therapist!

Therapy, Shmerapy

What I Want to Be When I Grow Up

I was a therapist long before I was a social worker.

How old was I, you want to know?

Maybe eight? Ten? For sure by the time I was bas mitzvah. When girls in camp confided in me their little secrets and problems, when girls in my class whispered to me their tears. When I became aware that everything hurt inside of me; I acutely felt the pain of those around me.

I was a sensitive radar picking up signals that were like so many tiny electric shocks to my system. The old lady who sat on her porch across the street, her face wistful with longing for her grown children to come visit. The child in the carriage crying, black streaks across his face, as his mother sat indifferently on the stoop at the corner of our block where our Hispanic neighbors gathered on sweaty summer nights. My teacher's mother who beamed with joy when we brazenly strolled into her home one Shabbos, not knowing that her daughter could not discipline the class; that we ran wild and made her cry. My classmate Esther, whose thin, shadow-like presence was wounding; her grief at her brother's illness shrouding her, arousing protectiveness in me.

In high school, I was a magnet for more secrets. And I held them all.

Sometimes, I should have told, but I did not know whom to tell, what to tell, how to tell. Some secrets were terrible secrets, so terrible that we knew adults could not know. That they would not believe or know what to do. But we, too, did not know what to do. So we talked. And I listened. And we talked some more. And sometimes, my classmates felt better.

In my school days, therapy did not exist. Or maybe it did, but it was a foreign world. It was not our world. When we begged our school to give us a psychology elective, a ripple of shock passed through the offices of the principals. Heresy! *Apikorsus*! We had no idea what psychology was, even when in twelfth grade we were assigned to uncover the psychology in Shakespeare's plays.

Girls who misbehaved were perpetually in the principal's office. Nobody thought their misbehavior meant anything. Who thought to discuss it with parents? Even when girls were failing, or cutting class. Or sitting alone during recess. Or refusing to show up for the school Shabbos. In my eighth grade class, there was one row called the Dumb Row. I do not know if the teacher knew about this subtle cruelty, but her despairing, sometimes mocking attitude toward the girls in the row validated their nickname, and subtly encouraged the class' behavior.

I grew up. Somewhat. And somewhere along the way entered college. I finished my bachelor's when my oldest was sixteen, just as an all-female school for social work opened its doors for the first time.

I walked inside and knew I had come home.

I belong to a listserv of religious mental health professionals, all members of Nefesh International. I belong to another listserv of doctors and therapist specifically working with clients who have severe trauma, namely clients with Dissasociative Identity Disorders (DID). As diverse as we are in our fields of psychology, mental health counseling, or social work, as different as the clients we see or the communities in which we practice, or as varied as our individual personalities, there is a common thread that unites most therapists.

There is a passion to help others, a vision of altruism that transcends our work, a driving ambition to make a difference, to right injustice, to connect to people, and even a constant desire to learn more and more and more so we can help more and more.

True, therapists make mistakes, and sometimes we *are* sensitive, on the defensive, arrogant, or missing the point. It is very true that we are human. But our similarities, these commonalities are often striking. I would venture to say, as I often do, that most therapists become therapists out of a history of their own pain. And therapists often make meaning of their pain by helping others, by leading others out of the tunnel of *their* pain.

How many of us are amused when our own clients, as if struck out of the blue, tell us, "I think I want to become a therapist!" And many of them do. (And even if the others don't, often we can determine the turning point of therapy when our clients not only are able to think past their pain, but begin to channel their pain, begin to find meaning in their experiences at the thought of helping others.)

That is why we are surprised over and over each time a client accuses us of not caring, of being motivated by the mercenary aspects of our field. Our passion for our work and the people in our lives and office so suffuses our entire beings that we are startled again and again when a client cannot feel our passion and our caring. And we laugh to think anybody can accuse us of being in this for the money, when we spend so many years working for almost the same pay as our cleaning ladies. And even then, we do not even dream that we will one day be in private practice. We are content to be swallowed up in our work; our payment is the satisfaction we get from it. For years we have done this work for free, with our classmates, neighbors, family, students, and random people who have called us for help. And now we are part of a like-minded community of other therapists, and it is exhilarating.

I know that is what it was like for me. What it is still like for me. And I know that so many of my colleagues feel the same.

We are starry-eyed and in love with our work.

We spend hours in training, reading, in supervision, attending conferences, buying new books, gadgets, and toys for our office with which to engage our clients.

We are humbled to be trusted in our client's journey.

And if you ask us, "Why did you become a therapist?" we will inevitably answer, "We did not become therapists; we were born this way."

PART I THE THERAPIST

Who's Who in Therapy

I recently attended the Nefesh Conference.
Whew.
Lots of fun. Lots of new information. Lots of new people!

Nefesh International is a Jewish, Orthodox organization for professionals in the field of mental health (like me), and rabbis who are involved with the issues our communities are confronted with daily. Believe it or not, Nefesh spans the world and has branches not only in the United States, but also in England, Brazil, Belgium, Argentina, and Israel.

Nefesh is great because it offers many training opportunities for therapists to continue learning and acquiring knowledge about the latest, most up-to-date therapies and techniques available for therapists. It also has a bi-annual weekend conference (that I just returned from) in which attendees get to meet an incredibly diverse group of Jewish religious social workers, psychologists, mental health professionals, psychiatric nurses, and psychiatrists. Other attendees — and Nefesh members — include rabbis, pastoral counselors, *mechanchim/mechanchos*, attorneys, coaches, and graduate students in the aforementioned fields. It's amazing!

What's the purpose of Nefesh?

It's to unite all these various fields to work together to address the diverse issues our fellow Jews — adults and children — face in the mental health arena, using the most cutting-edge information, training, and skills to improve the overall functioning of our schools, yeshivos, and communities. And all of this is done under the halachic guidance of the

Rabbanim in this organization, as well as the understanding that all *frum* professionals have a practice guided by Torah values and proper *guidance*. It's a wonderful organization, and I had a fabulous Shabbos.

But why am I talking about Nefesh?

Because as I was looking around at all the participants, I realized my readers may be interested to know what the difference is between all the letters after the names of the professionals, and why it makes a difference to begin with.

So here goes (and you can refer to the list detailed a few paragraphs prior):

Social workers (like me), psychologists, psychiatric nurses, and mental health professionals are all similar in that their schooling is at a master's level: i.e., after completing their BA degree, there are another two years of schooling for about sixty credits. (The differentiations to which I'm referring are for licensing in New York State. There are variations in the rest of the United States and possibly others outside of the USA.)

All degrees require many hours of practical work in the field of mental health, and all have licensing exams after those hours and classes are completed. Furthermore, all require additional supervised hours after graduating before being able to practice privately.

It is possible to obtain a social work degree through a bachelor's program, but these are not the therapists one would see in the traditional sense of therapy. In addition, psychologists often have additional years of training, usually a total of five years of schooling instead of two years, and obtain their doctorate. So the letters after their name would be Psy.D, meaning a doctorate in psychology. And they would be allowed to call themselves (and they do!) Dr. So-and-So.

Although it is hard to distinguish what makes someone a social worker versus a psychologist, psychiatric nurse, or mental health professional except for the actual letters that differ (LMSW/LCSW, Psychologist/PsyD, PMHNP or LMHP), the schooling itself differs in focus. Social workers are taught to view a person's problems through a social model, often referred to Person-in-Environment (PIE). Advocacy, social justice, and collaborating with all the systems in which a person lives are a part of social work values.

Psychologists are trained from a medical model and view a client's problems within the focus of a diagnosis found in the DSM-V, a manual that lists all mental health disorders. Although for insurance purposes, all mental health providers must give a diagnosis for reimbursement, for the psychologist it's more than a formality; it's how they are trained. Psychologists also are trained to do psychological evaluations, like IQ tests and all the other testing that would be required by, say, the Board of Education in order for a child to be found eligible for special education or gifted services.

Psychiatric nurses are those who have a bachelor's degree in nursing and go on to advanced training to be able to work in a hospital and other medical settings to assess, diagnose, and apply treatment. They can also do clinical work, working from a medical model of treatment.

The focus of schooling for the mental health professionals is clinical work. While both social workers and psychologists do clinical work, classes for mental health professionals do not focus on testing or on social issues, but mainly on clinical practice, in contrast to the prior two, in which clinical practice is limited to a much smaller number of classes.

Social workers can choose to work in administrative positions or other positions unrelated to direct clinical practice (therapy as we commonly call it), psychiatric nurses are advanced nurses who can prescribe medication in some states, and psychologists can do evaluations. Mental health professionals primarily do clinical work (therapy).

In the end, when all four end up as therapists working with individuals, couples, and families, they may look very similar, and they often are. The differences between them would depend on their post-graduate training, where their passion for counseling lies (children, teens, adults, or seniors; individuals or couple counseling), specific areas of expertise (like drug addiction counseling, play therapy, eating disorders, or anxiety disorders), and their theoretical orientation (attachment, cognitive behavioral, psychodynamic, gestalt, or family systems, to name a few).

Choosing a therapist has less to do with finding out which program they entered and more to do with their licensing (in contrast to unlicensed counselors), level of experience, post-graduate training, ongoing supervision and training, commitment to their work, and personality.

It's important that the therapist you choose is licensed because it not only means she or he has successfully completed all the requirements of their field, but also that the therapist has accountability to a licensing board in terms of ethical practice and confidentiality, as well as other aspects of therapy.

For the most part, psychiatrists, who are doctors (having completed the full, arduous, lengthy, and costly schooling of becoming a doctor), assess, diagnose, and prescribe medications, working collaboratively with therapists. Usually they do not do the clinical work, although they might incorporate a bit of counseling into their sessions with clients. Honestly? They are simply too expensive, generally, for most people to see on a weekly or even bi-weekly basis, and so their practice is usually limited to monthly, bi-monthly, or even visits less frequently, to administer medications for various mental health issues.

So there you have it.

Now imagine over five hundred therapists under one roof for four days straight.

A little crazy, no?

Definitely. But such fun!

When Talk Is Cheap, Is It Worth It?

It seems rather drastic.

I mean, the couple just got married and is having a little issue or two. You don't need a therapist for that, for goodness' sake. A little chat with the *Rav* or a *kallah* teacher, a little common sense, a little compromise, and all is good as new.

You don't need to run to a therapist for every little thing.

Maybe not. But this article explains how our ignorance of the role of a helping professional impacts negatively on those who need help.

To be very clear: Problems are not necessarily related to purposefully wanting to hurt another person. Dysfunction can emerge when a person lacks support, tools, or insight which causes a breakdown in acceptable and appropriate behavior and adversely shapes communication and relationships in the family, the school, the workplace, or in the greater community. This can happen when a mother is overwhelmed with the demands of an ill child, a father loses a job, a child is struggling socially or academically in school, and a myriad of other examples.

This is the typical cycle that happens in our community:

As our community generally balks at seeing a therapist, we first turn to our front-line leaders when there is a problem because there is no stigma attached. The *chassan* or *kallah* teacher, the *mechaneches* or involved neighbor, the Rav of the shul, or a non-professional coach or mentor-like individual who has an interest and talent for helping others.

But here is the distinction I would like to make between the help these special people offer versus what a therapist does. And why they should remain the front-line leaders to direct and consult, and not become the foot soldiers in the trenches actually fighting the war.

When a person reaches out for help, they belong in one of two categories. Either their problem is solution-oriented and can be successfully addressed by any intelligent, caring person within an hour or two, or the problem is deeply rooted and needs more time.

A couple has a disagreement about how to handle money that is threatening their *shalom bayis*. They consult a Rav, who gives them common-sense, direct solutions, and ways to compromise on their specific issue. The couple leaves and implements these ideas with much success. The issue is an issue no more.

Another couple approaches the Rav for what appears to be a similar issue. The Rav implements the same common-sense approach with solutions for compromise. The couple leaves but is back a day, even a week, later, unable to either implement the Rav's sage advice or with a fresh issue that needs to be discussed.

This scenario plays itself out with the helpful neighbor, the involved teacher, the non-professional mentor/counselor, and an assortment of others who try to get involved.

It doesn't work.

Therapy is not a feel-good, do-good, common-sense type of intervention that just any smart, caring person can do. There's a reason why a social worker, for example, is required to complete a minimum of two years of postgraduate school, which includes over a thousand hours of hands-on experience; another two thousand hours of supervised clinical work; and continuing education to maintain a licensed clinical degree.

An individual, couple, or family should be referred to a licensed professional if it is clear that the problem extends beyond a session or two of a Rabbi's or teacher's time.

Because *when a person is in crisis, change is most likely to occur.*

When a person reaches out for assistance, the person is most likely to pursue the help needed to alleviate the acute distress that has motivated him to seek the support in the first place. Once the individual's distress decreases, no matter how minimally, the motivation to seek assistance decreases as well.

One of the most powerful tools a therapist has is the self. The authentic, genuine, empathic self. A therapeutic alliance is what allows the therapist to use his repertoire of skills and interventions to effect positive change in a client. Since Rabbanim, teachers, mentors, and others who want to help often have many of the qualities a therapist has, *excluding an education and experience with therapy*, this alliance is created first with the non-professional helper. By the time this helper realizes that professional intervention is needed, the person in distress refuses to accept a referral. The individual is often unable to connect to a new person, and the therapy has been severely compromised in the absence of this crucial therapeutic alliance.

If the referral is made during the time of crisis, and before an attachment forms with the non-professional, the individual has the greatest chance of doing the work needed in therapy to effect change and develop healthy functioning.

There is a caveat I would like to address, a question that many people ask. What about life coaches or the like? They are not licensed professionals, but they *have* helped many people who can attest to their efficacy. Here is my answer. There are always some individuals who are unique, who are self-educated, who are pioneers in an untried field, who are innovative and creative. And there may be unlicensed professionals, coaches or others, who fall into this category.

But it would be imprudent to entrust your own, or a loved one's mental health into the hands of anyone, licensed or otherwise, who does not adhere to the strictest standards of professionalism. Furthermore, a non-licensed individual, in contrast to a licensed professional, has no licensing body to answer to in terms of how they conduct their services. This allows them to use interventions or apply treatment without consequences. Specifically, they can "practice" without having to report to anybody as far as their need for supervision or their need for ongoing education. In addition, nobody is checking up on them to ensure that they don't breach boundaries or clients' confidentiality.

And what is saddest is that when people reach out for help and are disillusioned with the help of non-professionals, they are burned out from seeking any help, thinking they have already tried everything, and not understanding how therapy is different.

PART I THE THERAPIST

Who Am I? Ethics in the Therapy Room

The teenager sitting in my office is violating Shabbos. Eats *treif*. Wants to wear pants instead of a skirt.

The couple coming to me for marital counseling is in pain. They are the sweetest people and want desperately to make their marriage work. But he is a *Kohen,* and she is a divorcee.

For another client, obsessive-compulsive behavior is manifesting itself in a distortion of matters we hold sacred, doing things like obsessively trying to rid her already *chametz*-free home from *chametz* before Pesach or accepting out-of-reach *kabbalos* upon herself in times of challenge.

A child describes his attempts to adhere to the commandment of *honor thy father,* but the description of his father's behavior indicates a mental illness that is wreaking havoc on the child's own ability to maintain mental stability.

Many decades ago, when I was a high school student, my friends and I begged for some courses in psychology. The school administration was horrified. "*Apikorsus!*" they exclaimed.

And yet today, many upstanding religious high schools offer courses in psychology.

In my days, the premise of psychology and therapy was heresy. The doctrines, the philosophy, the teachings were all based on the theories of Sigmund Freud, the father of psychology.

Today psychology has branched out, and Freud's disciples have long since abandoned his teachings in favor of psychology that teaches the importance and impact of human relationships, that emphasizes human development in the context of those relationships, both positive and negative. Today there are many theories and methods of psychological treatment that can be seamlessly integrated into our Torah lifestyle and value systems. When I went to college to become a social worker, I do not remember struggling with religious beliefs in context of the courses I was obligated to take.

But yet today as a therapist, I struggle.

In the context of my practice, who am I first? A social worker — or a religious Jew?

This question becomes even harder to answer when I sit with a client and religious values clash in the context of the therapeutic setting.

Here is why.

As a social worker, I am bound by the Code of Ethics that charges me to be "culturally competent." According to section 1.05(b), I must seek to understand social diversity with respect to religious and/or cultural differences, and according to (c) I may not exploit others to further my own religious interests.

So how do I counsel that teen who is violating the Shabbos? As a therapist I am fully present with her in her pain and do not seek to foist my values on her, but I am moved to help her discover her own path; on the other hand, as a religious Jew, it pierces me to my core and I want her to find *Yiddishkeit* again. In a different setting, how do I respond to the teen coming from a far more religious background who asks me about going to college when it is clearly against her cultural upbringing?

How do I counsel a couple whose very marriage defies *halachah*? Can I be a party to effect the success of a marriage between two people the Torah forbids in marriage?

How do I straddle the fence between what psychologically appears to be my client's needs and yet seemingly clear halachic violations of Honor thy Father and Mother? We all know the story of the *tzaddik* who allowed his mentally ill mother to shame him in public and even bent over to become a step-stool as she walked on his back over the mud. Is that what is expected of our clients when faced with similar challenges?

As a social worker I am bound by the Code of Ethics to be committed to the client, to allow for self-determination and not advance my own agenda. I must display cultural competency and resolve conflicts of interest in ways that respect the client's needs more than my own.

As a religous Jew, sometimes the Code of Ethics creates seemingly insurmountable conflicts between what is perceived as right for the client and what is right for a Jew.

And here is what I do, to the best of my ability.

Sometimes, I put it right out there for my clients who are less observant than I am or struggle religiously. I say, "You realize from my dress and wig that I am religious. Are you okay with that?" That may open up a discussion of how they are afraid of being judged on their own lifestyle, which they feel is incongruous to mine.

I say, "Look, I am a therapist and my job is to help you solve the problems that brought you here to begin with. I am not judging you or pushing religion on you. But the same way being a woman influences the way I think; being a New Yorker has impacted who I am; being a religious Jew has also been a causative factor in my makeup. I am a person here in this room, as you are. And I intend to relate to you as a person, not as a robot. So if you ever feel judged by my views, hey, let me know, and it will be part of our work together!"

But then there are situations which truly seem to violate my religious — or ethical — values.

If the issue is mine alone — like counseling a couple who is not allowed to be together halachically — and I want to know what the *psak*, the ruling, is for me as a therapist (as the couple finds *halachah* irrelevant), I have a Rav to whom I will pose my questions.

If the client wants halachic guidance regarding matters brought up in therapy, I encourage him to sign a release allowing me to talk to his Rabbi, and then help him submit his questions for clarification.

I cannot recall a time when there was no satisfactory, Torah-true solution to a dilemma that appeared to be a conflict between ethical and religious values.

Because in truth, the no-brainer is that we do the best we can and the rest is up to G-d.

Therapy, Shmerapy

Yes, Even Therapists Need Therapists!

Here's a secret about therapy:

Therapists often meet with supervisors.

Here's a common scenario (although for reasons of confidentiality, I am using a scenario that has *never* occurred — yet!):

I walk into my supervisor's office one day.

"I don't know what to do about Client X," I say between clenched teeth.

"Sit down," my supervisor says. She knows me for years and doesn't get fazed by my intensity. "Relax. What's going on?"

I laugh. "It's my client, Mr. X. He is my first appointment on Fridays, and I am late every week. I even leave the house early, and something always happens to make me late. Or I walk in by the skin of my teeth, panting from running to get there on time. It's driving me crazy."

Let me explain what supervision is all about.

All responsible therapists go for regularly scheduled meetings with a supervisor. Weekly, monthly, bi-monthly. Whichever. A therapist can pay for supervision or can join a peer-supervision group. Some therapists do both, or even have multiple supervisors to guide them in different aspects of their practice. So if a therapist works with disabled children, and also with adult survivors of abuse, she may go for supervision to receive guidance specific to disabilities in children, as well as a second course of supervision addressing the impact of abuse in adults. Supervision is ongoing training for a therapist. In my opinion, and in the opinion of those seasoned professionals that I trust, you (okay, not you, but me) are never too experienced or too good for supervision. Or at least, a responsible therapist always feels he/she is in a constant flux of learning (although supervision is in addition to ongoing training that, again, any responsible therapist makes it her business to attend on a pretty regular basis).

A newly graduated and licensed social worker (LMSW) needs a minimum of two thousand hours of clinical work within six years, plus almost weekly supervision before she can apply for her clinical license (LCSW). Personally, I would not touch a therapist who ever stops going for supervision even if he/she is in the field over thirty years. Therapy is very personal work in which the therapist's self is a crucial tool in therapy. Since that is the case, the therapist's self needs to constantly be in training to keep up with the times and with the program. Any therapist who thinks his/her self is perfect is not one who I would trust to perfect mine in therapy!

Many states require a certain amount of training credits to be acquired over a two-year period in order to maintain a social work license, although any self-respecting therapist will attend this training without that state requirement anyway. While training and workshops keep therapists informed about the newest ideas, interventions, and updated information, supervision helps to keep the therapist's inner self grounded so that the daily grind of listening to problems and perhaps experiencing trauma vicariously does not impair her ability to be present and effective. Supervision also gives the therapist insight into how she functions as a therapist and where her pitfalls are when working with specific populations and problems. It helps take away any blind spots in her vision when in the driver's seat of the therapist's chair.

Although supervision is not therapy, there are very interesting studies that show how the client-therapist alliance sometimes goes through a similar pattern that is enacted between supervisor and therapist.

So here I am struggling with Mr. X and my unnerving problem of showing up late — or almost late — for our appointments despite my

Therapy, Shmerapy

protestations that I leave my house in a timely manner.

Who are we kidding? I know, because when a client of mine arrives late, even if only once, my antennas are up wondering what subconscious forces are at play that makes my client, despite his/her protestations, resistant to therapy that is manifesting itself in lateness?

So here is how supervision works:

Depending on years of experience and knowledge, my supervisor may talk about therapeutic concepts of resistance, transference, counter-transference, and/or defenses. Then my supervisor will use different methods, be it Socratic questioning, confrontation, or discussion to help me understand the forces that make me want to avoid therapy with this client.

And because supervision is fascinating, fun, and frustrating, I may learn a few things about myself that have been lurking in my blind spot.

Maybe I have been avoiding Mr. X because he reminds me of someone in my past that I disliked immensely (my ninth-grade math teacher)? Maybe because I feel ineffective in helping him solve his problems, and instead of dealing with my feelings of helplessness, I choose to run away (or come late?). Or maybe the issue is simply because he brings a body odor into the room that I don't know how to handle.

So my supervisor will model for me effective therapy tools that I will learn and pass on to my clients. She will help me build awareness of how my dislike of him may be rooted in my dislike of someone he reminds me of, that it really has nothing to do with him. And that needs to be addressed so I can see him for who he is: a person in pain who needs my help, so that I can genuinely like him and respect him. She will build on my strengths and help me uncover ways in which I can destroy those helpless feelings that I have, and probably he has, as well, so I can empower myself and him to improve his life in ways which are important to him. She will trust me to figure out ways in which I can either help him with hygiene, or cope with the odor if it would not be in his best interests to become aware of how his odor affects me at this time.

And the funny thing is, although I may not be aware of it, my supervisor may be talking to *her* supervisor how she barely comes to sessions with *me* on time, and she doesn't know why it's happening. And *her* supervisor may help *her* uncover her reasons for avoidance… and then we all live happily ever after.

So now you know another therapy secret.

You gonna be on time next session?

Therapy, Shmerapy

Bloopers: Mistakes I Have Made as a Therapist

Therapists are human. Have I mentioned that before? If I didn't, then this must come as a huge surprise to the many clients who expect their therapists to be perfect. And I will take a deep breath here (deep breath, count in for four and out for seven... whoosh... and again....) and confess that I have made many mistakes as a therapist. And I have been humbled by those mistakes, learned from them, and sometimes even celebrated them. So in no special order, here goes.

My head on a platter, for you to do with it as you please.

(And, of course, all my clients detailed below gave me permission to share...)

Once, I scheduled a new client for an evening appointment. My client's father made the appointment for his daughter. I wrote it in my appointment book and closed the book. No sweat, right? Wrong. I scheduled three clients for a night I had no intention of working. And she was my first of those three. So there I was, coming back from a wedding, and my phone rang once, twice, three times. It was my client's father, wondering where I was because his daughter was outside my office, ringing my bell. Totally confused, I checked my book, and there were the appointments in black and white. I was horrified and apologized to her father, rescheduled her appointment (I can't believe she still wanted to see me), and of course, waived the fee for that first appointment to express my sincere apologies. And then I ran to the office to meet my next two clients, looking a little too elegant for the appointment, but whatever...

When that same client showed up for the first time — again — and I apologized once more, telling her this had never happened to me before, she said wearily, "It's okay. These things *always* happen to me." Her posture and droopy shoulders screamed, "I am just so insignificant that I am overlooked."

And that was the beginning of an excellent run of therapy in which my mistake became the catalyst to show her that she is in charge of her own destiny, and while these things may happen, she can make things happen as well. Which she has. Most remarkably.

Here's another.

Watching one's therapist yawning is probably one of the most invalidating, traumatic events that can happen to a client in therapy. Guilty. Guilty. Guilty.

At a recent conference I attended, a presenter gave an incredible workshop on this topic of therapeutic mistakes I raised my hand and said, "I have a client that I respect tremendously for her courageous and honest work. And yet, when I am with her in session, I find myself yawning. I can't even apologize because I don't know if it won't happen again. It's not necessarily that I am tired, because during the session right before, and directly after, I don't yawn — not even once. I don't even have the *urge* to yawn. It's driving me crazy because it's such a terrible thing for me to do!"

"Is she boring you?" the presenter asked. "Because then it can give insight into her interactions with others that may be affecting her socially."

I said, "No. She is not boring nor does she bore me, although I do sometimes feel a heaviness in the room that makes me sleepy."

"Is she depressed?" Janice asked.

"Yes," I said. "She's down a lot."

"Then maybe let her know," the presenter said, "how you are yawning because her sadness is pervading the session and you can finally get a glimpse of the heaviness she feels that makes it so hard for her to get through the day."

I went back into the session, apologized for my yawning, and told my client about the exchange I had had at the conference workshop.

Today I feel my clients' pain more deeply than ever before — especially with those with whom I find myself yawning in session.

Big confession here. When I was an intern, six months after I began my Master's in Social Work, I hugged my client. (Shocked you, right? Wait till you get to the chapter entitled "Hoopla About the Hug!") I didn't dare tell my supervisor because when I nervously, yet casually, broached the subject and asked her if it's ever appropriate to hug a client, her face was such a mask of horrification (yes, I made up that word because it best describes her facial distortions), I knew enough not to admit to such a terrible deed. But I did hug my client. She was an aristocratic, regal woman, over 100 years old, who had survived not only the Holocaust, but had outlived some of her children. Her home was immaculate, she prayed daily, her clothing was starched and elegant, and her silver gleamed in the china closet.

I was a young novice sent to her home to assess it for safety after her discharge from a hospital stay. I have no idea who made that decision because forget about *her* safety; *I* felt safe in her presence. A woman who survived until now with such grace and faith was one with whom I felt safe enough to face the world with all the troubles I would soon be listening to. And when I said my goodbye at the door, I don't know what came over me, but I simply reached out to give her a hug. Maybe to take a hug.

Unprofessional. Totally.

I have never told anyone this. Except you — the thousands of readers reading this! My confessions don't even begin to cover the times my clients talk about difficulties they are having in relationships, and I have just seen my own child explain to me that his mother — his social worker mother — is so impossible to deal with because I ask him so many questions about his life... (I know, I know... he's a teenager. I tell that to my clients, but I need somebody to tell me!)

Sometimes, though, I only *think* I make mistakes.

New client. She never showed up for her session. She made that first appointment and then simply canceled the day before. No explanation.

I tried to understand where I went wrong. Was I abrupt on the initial phone call? Should I have encouraged her to explain more fully her reason for coming? Alleviated her fears about trying therapy? Should I have avoided/responded to her question about my age, background, schooling, degree, religious affiliation, if it's true I am related to Person X, or any other curve ball I sometimes get? Was money the issue and I should have referred her to an agency?

Years later, I received an email. "I read your articles in *Binah* and don't know if you remember me," a woman wrote, and she went on to jog my memory with details of her call to me, "but I wanted to let you know what happened."

I did remember her because she was one of my first *almost* clients in private practice.

"When I told my husband I finally made the appointment," she continued, "he was so shocked at how desperate I was that he finally began to take me seriously and we began to work things out. That phone call was life-changing for our marriage. Thank you so much for helping me have the guts to schedule the appointment and then not making a fuss when I canceled."

So there you have it. Imperfection. The illusion of your therapist's life perfectly lived, stripped away.

Thank you for trusting me anyway.

Part II
The Client

Safety. The second floor of the pyramid.

My client needs to be safe. She cannot care about anything while bombs are falling. Bombs of war from where she hides in her bomb shelter, bombs of fists or words from where she hides under her covers in her room. She needs freedom from fear of abuse, whether the battle is driven by terrorists or her parents; or even if there is transgenerational trauma in which the fears of her parent(s) are transmitted although the war has long since been over.

The need for safety means financial security; it means not to fear illness or death; to feel safe against accidents. Although none of these are absolute, a person must be able to experience some level of safety in these areas.

My client quotes the poet A.E Housman: "I am a stranger and afraid/in a world I never made," and tells me how she has always felt afraid at home with her bullying brother, unprotected by her parents.

Another describes the chaos that surrounded her, rules of family, school, and religion that made no sense to her.

"I lived within systems
that if I wouldn't have broken every rule
I would have been buried beneath them."

And the celebration of a teacher who cared to make her feel safe...

"As a teenager, I felt like I was a skydiver,
hurtling towards the rocks without a parachute,
ready to smash against those rocks,
into a thousand pieces.

My teacher opened the parachute. I felt I could breathe—
The parachute was damaged; I was still heading towards the rocks, but at least now I had some breathing room."

I remember reading these beautiful words by D.W. Winnicott, an English pediatrician and psychoanalyst, observing the safety created by the *good-enough* mother, despite the inherent dangers of growing up: "A baby supports himself by arms that do not hold him... In the moment he is emphasizing his need for Mother, he is proving he can do without her, because he is walking alone."

Defense Mechanisms

"She's in total denial. Not that I blame her. Who wants to deal with such a problem?"

Recognize that line?

She — whoever that *she* is in your life — is in denial about any number of things. That her daughter bullies others at school, that her son needs tutoring, that she is too picky about *shidduchim*, that her mother is very ill, that her house is a mess, that she is a lousy cook.

Or how about this line?

"So what if I wore the outfit once and then returned it? The department store doesn't sell returns anyway."

Both of these lines indicate a defense mechanism at play. The first is **denial** (refusing to face an issue), the second is **rationalization** (justifying actions with reasons that obscure the real motives — here that the person is committing theft, whichever way you slice it).

If you were wondering, here's the answer to your question: No, I am not a therapist outside of my office. I do not examine your behavior in the supermarket or at the shoemaker. No, I do not analyze you at the pool or park. And I do not even remotely study you or pass judgment on you in any social or other setting, or consider whether or not you could use therapy.

I walk out of my therapy room, and I become the most clueless, unobservant, and unperceptive person, noticing nothing, happily oblivious to what anyone else is thinking, doing, wearing, or feeling.

But if I choose to, I can know you better than you know yourself by how you reveal yourself through your defense mechanisms.

In psychological babble, a *defense mechanism* is a subconscious way we protect ourselves from anxiety-provoking situations. And there are many of them in addition to the two mentioned above.

Defense mechanisms are different from the healthy coping mechanisms we use in tough situations in a few ways. Defenses operate mostly outside of consciousness, while coping tools are rooted in the conscious, in the here-and-now. Defenses feel automatic, as if driven by something outside of us that compels us to act that way even when we hate this seemingly automatic behavior. While true coping tools are oriented to reality, defenses distort the present and are driven by the past. Defenses ease anxiety with impulse gratification, subterfuge, attempting to create a smokescreen for the real issue at hand; its main goal is to remove the disturbing affect, *not* solve the problem. Healthy coping involves choice, purposefulness, openness, and an ability to tolerate an uncomfortable situation in order to resolve it.

It's the defense mechanisms a person uses — or doesn't need to use — that allows a therapist, even one outside the office, to read a person with something tantamount to x-ray vision.

Even untrained people who have a gift for being attuned to others are able to interpret behaviors. So if you are one of these socially gifted individuals, this article will simply identify one of the tools in your repertoire — understanding the defenses people use and why.

After you read about a few defenses, you may either be squirming in your seat, or couch, or wherever you are reading this because you recognize yourself, or you are enjoying the new understanding it gives you when dealing with your parent, child, workmate, or husband.

Ready? Here goes.

You come home from work and your kid's briefcase is on the floor right by the door when you have told him a million times to put it away when he comes home from school. And you give it to him good. Your yelling can be heard out the window and down the block all the way to Kalamazoo. Yes, leaving a briefcase in the hallway is irritating, but it has not become a capital offense yet. Chances are what you are doing is **displacement.** You really want to be yelling at your workmate or boss, but can't; instead, the safest person to yell at is your seven-year-old.

It's weird when your sister-in-law tells you, "My neighbor has her *hashkafos* twisted. She lets her husband work twenty hours a day, and doesn't say a word, even when he arrives to the block after the first siren Erev Shabbos," when everyone knows her own husband is a workaholic. She is using **projection**, attributing unacceptable thoughts and feelings onto others, denying they belong to her, pretending she does not feel similarly.

But defenses may not necessarily be negative.

Here's a great one to use because it channels socially unacceptable impulses in a positive direction, much in the same way we were taught that when someone enjoys bloodshed, they should become a *shochet*. It's called **sublimation**. A person who relishes control may become a doctor, principal, or CEO. (Hmm, so you are wondering what sublimation is at work when someone becomes a therapist?)

Or what Yosef Hatzaddik did in Egypt when he avoided sinning because of the vision of his father before his eyes. That is **internalization** — when we incorporate other people into our very being and make them part of us to avoid dealing with something alone. Internalization is in play when we make wise decisions about child-rearing by hearing our mother's voice inside our head.

The negative aspect of **internalization** is when we swallow the other person whole and lose ourselves in the process, when we make decisions that are not our own because of our anxiety that must be avoided at all costs. It's sometimes seen in how girls come back from seminary looking and acting like clones of their teachers (although this too can be part of a normal spiritual developmental process).

Repression, identification, introjection, internationalization, fantasy, idealization, regression, somatization, splitting, compensation, undoing, withdrawal... so many defenses. So little time to cover them all!

Therapy, Shmerapy

Enigma of Stigma

Maybe you will recognize yourself in this article.

Maybe you will recognize someone else you know: a child, a spouse, a parent, or a student.

Then, maybe once you recognize that person, stuff about therapy will make more sense to you. The stigma of therapy will seem silly to you. You might turn to your newlywed wife and ask curiously, "Have you ever gone to therapy?" And if she will say yes, you will be jealous. Therapy will seem like a treat you also want to experience.

Who lands up in therapy?

Forty years ago, in our community, the answer would have been crazy people. Really messed up individuals and families.

"So, really, Mindy," you want to know, "who lands up in therapy?"

The answer is very different today, and most people know the right answer.

It's your neighbor. Your son. Your daughter's high school teacher. Your spouse. The guy that fixes your plumbing and charges you a fortune. It's that woman you always meet in the café who is dressed to the nines and the guy your husband learns with every night. A principal, a CEO, the electrician, the philanthropist; a struggling mother, a bullied daughter, the anxious father, the grieving spouse.

You.

You are the kind of person who lands up in therapy.

A normal person who has friends and a job; knows how to laugh and organize; is a perfectly ordinary human being who has her regular

Tehillim group or *shiur*, who is involved in *chessed* activities, who is the *gabbai* in shul or the *menahel* of a prestigious yeshivah. That's who.

What are you doing in therapy?

Lounging around on my couch and drinking coffee.

No, I'm just kidding. But if you laughed then you either recognize yourself in that description or you simply have a good sense of humor. And that's just part of your ordinariness, part of the ordinariness of most people who enter therapy.

People today enter therapy because they are struggling with some issue that is impacting their life is some way, and the same way they would take would use some sort of remedy for that annoying foot fungus, they choose to take care of their mind fungus as well.

Anxiety, fears, trauma, and grief. Bed-wetting, social skills, dating issues, and relationships. Hair pulling, rebelliousness, numbness, and anger management. Every human condition that causes us upset is a reason to enter therapy to alleviate the symptoms and distress and improve daily living and our relationships.

While it's true that our generation can little tolerate discomfort and that becomes a negative judgment on us, I choose to see the positive aspect of our lack of tolerance as the primary motivator for therapy. *I don't want to tolerate the fighting with my wife, the yelling at my kids, snapping at my workmates; I don't want to tolerate living with fears of flying, of leaving my house, of germs. So I will do something to take it away.*

While a spouse in a previous generation might have learned to tolerate excessive stinginess in a marriage, abandon all hope for change, and learn manipulative or sly ways of hiding money from that controlling spouse, a spouse today would rather establish appropriate boundaries and behavior, improve the relationship, and create a home in which there are no secrets, lies, or anger.

Today's parents don't accept the inevitability of their sweet or quirky child being bullied in school, they don't accept their socially inept child's lack of friends as unavoidable, and they expect — rightly so — that there

Therapy, Shmerapy

must be ways to help their child acquire tools to live happier and more successful lives. Spouses, while hopefully understanding, don't write off their partner's phobias of germs or flying in an airplane as status quo — they encourage them to get help so that they can visit their children in who are studying in Israel together as a couple, so that their home can be an emotionally safe place.

If that low tolerance for discomfort breeds an attitude that accepts therapy, among other tools, as a means to improve one's ability to overcome limitations and improve character and relationships, I would venture to say that living in our generation has its definite benefits.

I have clients who make that first call to me independently, some as young as fifteen, while others are sent by their parents ten years into their marriage. Principals mandate therapy for their students, and concerned neighbors or friends exert pressure on loved ones. Married children send their parent who has lost a spouse and has deteriorated into depression, and a *Rav* sends parents with an unhappy child who is wrecking himself and others in his desperate unhappiness.

So sometimes, I have a client who has absolutely no idea — or so they say — as to why she needs therapy. And sometimes I have a client who knows she needs it but is unsure how therapy will help.

And most of my clients, once they sit down in my office, say, "I can't believe I am doing this therapy thing. I feel so weird. Even nutty," and I laugh and respond, "Join the club."

There are pretty few people left today who haven't had some contact with therapy.

So my clients, too, struggle with the stigma, even as they know they have no choice but to come. No choice because their spouse or school prinicpal has made therapy mandatory or because their situation seems so desperate that right now living with their problem seems much worse than living with the stigma of being in therapy.

It does not take long for my clients to acknowledge how the decision to enter therapy made sense. So the ones that have been forced to come see me, are secretly relieved — never admitting it, of course — that someone cared enough to force therapy upon them and the ones whose own feelings of desperation or discontent forced them through my door experience overwhelming relief that they had the courage to finally do it. And I am sure there are hundreds — no thousands — of clients seeing other therapists who feel similarly.

What would make seem much nuttier to me is sitting in a dark room within inches of a light switch, because you wonder what the blind bats — who have an aversion to light — would think of you if you switched on the light. Because bats are not really blind, you know. They just see differently. They navigate using their sense of sound. Therapy may *sound* like a stigma, but I prefer to see with my eyes. Then the view of therapy is a lot clearer.

Therapy, Shmerapy

Selfish in Therapy

What would you do if your daughter *whines* that she has to load the dishwasher every night after supper? Or if your son complains that he doesn't want to run his Friday errands anymore? How would you respond to yet another child who balks at visiting his grandfather each weekend, or to yet another who refuses to babysit when you need to leave to a wedding or funeral?

What would be your reaction to the mother who cries that she is sick of doing laundry or cooking supper? To the father who refuses to learn with his son each night? To the friend who says she is not giving out her notes to be photocopied by her best friend? To the married daughter who stops visiting her mother in the nursing home? To the brother who does not take part in family weddings?

Selfish! Selfish! Selfish! That would be the normal reaction. No?

Absolutely.

If my daughter would whine about the dishes, I would explain how everyone has a job to do in the house, and this is hers. I would say the same to the kid throwing a fit about babysitting or running errands.

I would be properly horrified by the mother who abdicates responsibility for supper and fresh laundry, by the father who washes his hands of learning with his sons, by the married daughter who flagrantly neglects the commandment to honor her mother.

But sometimes these individuals enter therapy, and soon, these may be the behaviors they are displaying.

It sounds like therapy contradicts everything we are taught about being a giving, selfless person, one reader wrote to me in an email.

And I totally get what she means.

It most certainly does look like that. It looks downright awful. Absolutely horrible that the changes that therapy bring allow a teenager to shirk his or her responsibilities in their home, for a parent to deny his or her children normalcy, for an ill mother to be left to languish alone in a nursing home without her daughter's care, or for a sibling to opt out of family celebrations like weddings and get-togethers.

But many readers are already so therapy-savvy that they can absolutely understand that in some cases, these behaviors can make sense in another context, in the context of the dysfunction that therapy seeks to alleviate. So there can be a therapeutically sound reason for a mother to stop making dinners for her family.

(You can't imagine what that can be? What if the mother is a single mother working to support her family and she lives with her three adult daughters, who each have only part-time jobs? What if the mother is the one who does all the laundry and cooking and cleaning, and the daughters refuse to take responsibility for the home despite the mother's constant entreaties? Hmmm. Makes more sense now, right? "Oh," you can now say knowingly. "The mother is enabling these selfish behaviors and needs to stop making dinner in order to restore functioning to the home." Good, you get it.)

And if you look at the examples at the start of this article, it is not hard to stretch your imagination to see where each of these behaviors can make sense. Such as that a ten-year-old should not be babysitting four younger children of varying ages whenever her parents need to go to a wedding. Or a child should not be forced to visit a grandparent who speaks abusively or is violent in some way, with the child unprotected in the grandparent's home. A friend needs to set boundaries if photocopying her notes inevitably means she doesn't get her notes back in time for her final. And a brother will not attend a wedding that his *Rav* has *paskened* is halachically inadvisable.

So we are clear here that tough times may call for tough measures, right?

But there is one person who cannot reconcile the concept of a religious Jew as a selfless, giving person and the Jew who needs to exercise her rights to be selfish. This is the person who is inherently selfless, trapped in someone else's selfishness, and cannot differentiate between normal and abnormal expectations and rules of behavior.

While she knows logically that it is patently unfair to have to load the dishwasher every night, bathe all the children, do homework with her siblings, and clean the kitchen after supper perfectly while her mother is out nightly volunteering for various organizations, she is so good that she feels guilty for even thinking of holding her mother back from her seemingly lofty activities and feels selfish for her angry and frustrated thoughts.

Therapy definitely does not contradict the Torah way of selflessness and giving.

When a person enters therapy and struggles with various issues, sometimes a therapist can see how boundary violations have occurred and continue to occur, and where the client may need to delineate those boundaries in a healthy way.

Sometimes, I need to help a client say no to a parent, say no to her child, say no to her friend, sibling, or spouse. And often, when clients who are inherently good and caring people are faced with having to engage in in behaviors that appear to directly oppose all they have learned from their teachers and *Rebbeim*, I encourage them to speak to their Rav. Sometimes, I will speak to their Rav with them, for them. Inevitably, the Rav will hear and agree with my assessment and plan of intervention.

Because you know the story of the mother who had had one egg and many starving children? She took the egg and ate it herself. Because she said, "You need a mother and I cannot be one if I am starving or dead of hunger."

And sometimes that is what therapy needs to do. Give the client permission to eat the entire apple by himself so he can be the person who will become the ultimate giver from a secure place of health, not starvation.

PART II THE CLIENT

Mandate Reporting

It is a therapist's worst nightmare.

Mine, at least.

The night before I begin therapy with a client under eighteen, I do not sleep well.

It is the specter of fear in having to report abuse to Child Protective Services.

Parents, teachers, and principals call me to take on their teenager or student as a client. The kid is acting out in all sorts of ways. Rebellious, angry, troublesome. Or withdrawn, depressed, disheveled. And these parents, teachers, and principals are worried. "Do something," they tell me. "Make her better." Or, "Find the daughter that I used to know. Bring back the student she used to be."

They tell me their worst fears. "But whatever you do, don't do what Therapist X did last year. You know, because of her, the children were taken out of the Z family! Because of Therapist Z, the Y teenager left home. Make sure that doesn't happen here, Mindy."

They want me to promise. And I wish I could.

But I can't.

Here is the truth: People think that Child Protective Services grabs children out of their homes, dumping them in foster care at the slightest pretense. Yeah, right.

I used to work in an agency. Often, my clients were referred to our agency by Child Protective Services (CPS) because of some sort of abuse that had occurred in their home. For the most part, these children remained at home, under the supervision of CPS, which left the child in the home, but came into the house to mandate services like therapy, demand that parents clean out the mold in the refrigerator, and make sure the child has adequate food each day and attends school.

A far cry from the snatch-and-kidnap vision we have of CPS.

A number of times, the director of my agency, after listening to me describe a home situation that concerned me, asked me to call CPS. For those of you who are unaware, there is an option I often exercise that entails calling CPS anonymously, presenting the case in question and asking if the described situation warrants CPS intervention. If yes, as a mandated reporter, I would be required to make a report. If not, I would obtain the name of the representative I was talking to, the date and time of our conversation, and record in the client's chart the content of our conversation, including the representative's assessment that this case does not warrant protective services at this time.

What is my point in sharing this with you?

To let you know that when a therapist calls Child Protective Services, and they come in to take away the children, there is a very strong reason that this has occurred!

Yes, it may have happened to the nicest family on your block; yes, you may think that a terrible travesty of justice has occurred; but it will not change one unalterable, inescapable fact: *Something terrible is suspected, there are adequate grounds for suspicion, and the therapist had no choice but to either save the child and potentially destroy herself or to stay silent to protect herself and potentially destroy the child.*

It's a horrible choice. It's a no-win legal and moral choice.

But therapists, along with doctors, police officers, licensed teachers, and other providers, paid or volunteer, in health care settings, are legally *mandated reporters*. And mandated reporters who fail to report suspected abuse or suspicion of the possibility of substantial risk of harm to a child can face a conviction of a Class A misdemeanor, which carries a sentence of up to one year in jail and/or a $1,000 fine, including being additionally sued for monetary damages for harm caused by failure to report, and possible revocation of his practicing license if a complaint is filed to the licensing board.

Whew.

And those of you outside the professional field think this kind of report happens randomly or indiscriminately.

Those of you outside of this field react with horror and disbelief at the actions of an agency or therapist who became a mandated reporter — not because the therapist loves talking on the phone — *but because something terrible may have occurred or continues to occur to the child in her care!*

I would challenge you to stop a minute and think if any therapist in our communities would be crazy enough to risk the wrath of the community, even her own family members, to risk her standing in the community, her job and livelihood, to risk being literally run out of town, to make this report if *she would not be absolutely sure* that it is a matter of life and death either/or physically, emotionally or mentally for her client.

Do you think she is that crazy?

I am definitely not.

That is why, although ultimately I must make the final decision whether or not I am mandated to legally report, and ultimately I must bear the burden of such a report should it have to be made, I optimally seek the guidance, with consent of course, of the Rav who is connected to the child's school, family, or greater community to ensure maximum protection and positive results for the child.

So when you hear of a therapist who made that call, when you hear of a child who left home, do me a favor: Instead of raging at the therapist who made the call the protect the child, why not steer your anger at the people in the child's life who have either failed to protect — or have harmed — that child?

(As of today, I have an unpublished number, disconnected email addresses, and have moved to an undisclosed location in the Witness Protection program, and so if you are out to get me, you will find me safe under my covers!)

Therapy, Shmerapy

Our Community Does Not Recognize Evil

Our small, close-knit communities are marvelous places in which to raise children. Often, within a radius of twenty or so blocks, children are near their grandparents, cousins, schools, synagogues, and assorted communal events they choose to attend. They are enveloped in the security of their close contact with their principals and teachers whom they meet in the synagogue, on the street, and sometimes even in the bungalow colony. They are surrounded not only by cousins at their schools and camps, but their parents' or aunts' friends, who become their counselors and teachers; by uncles and their friends, who sometimes become *rebbeim* or employers.

It is difficult for a child raised in such a warm, loving environment to envision any sort of evil. It is difficult for such a child to think that some children are scared of their parents' rages, do not receive dinner if they misbehave, are beaten by siblings, have lice that is neglected for months on end, are left alone to care for many younger siblings while their parents disappear for hours, and live in filthy homes where laundry piles up for weeks at a time. Such a child cannot envision a home that looks spotless yet breeds fear and a tense atmosphere because parents have personality disorders, mental disorders; a home where secrets must be kept at all costs to preserve a smooth artificial mask that hides horrific pain and horror.

But this article is not to talk about the child who cannot envision evil. It is to speak to the adults who cannot, and in their naiveté, help perpetuate the very evil that would shock their goodness.

As a social worker working with the mainstream *frum* community, I struggle with the very goodness of some of our prominent community leaders, people who are so good that they have no model of malevolence; hence, they inflict damage on those suffering in our midst. They end up protecting the perpetrators instead of the victims, thinking the victims must be spreading hoaxes by accusing their parents, their *rebbeim*, their older siblings of terrible crimes.

But how could they know the truth? The only truth in their lives is the wholesome goodness with which they have raised their children; they can envision no other way for a Torah-observant Jew to act.

I will give you a scenario culled from experience working with abuse in our community. I do not break confidentiality here because this is Nobody's story, yet Everybody's.

A teenager calls a teacher on the phone. The teacher can barely hear the child as she convulses in tears bordering on hysteria, choking out her frustration that she works so hard all day long at home, she is not allowed to join her friends after school, she must cook and clean and care for younger siblings. The child stammers, in her flood of tears, that she has been *mechallel Shabbos* because how can she believe in a Hashem Who allows such painful situations to occur?

The teacher is a seasoned *mechaneches*. She herself is a mother of many children. She knows how a house is run, how everyone has jobs, how sometimes the oldest child feels much pressure. She knows what a close relationship she has with her oldest daughter; she knows about the secrets they share, the privileges her oldest receives as thanks for her hard work. This teacher has counseled hundreds of girls who are grateful for her clear insight into the roles of daughters in *klal Yisrael* and who grow up fiercely proud of the roles they play in their homes, eager to perpetuate the warmth of their parents' homes into their own.

So this teacher begins to calm the girl down. No, it's not as bad as she is making it seem. She's exaggerating. Of course her mother loves her. She's sure this teenager is able to go out with friends often enough. This is her

Therapy, Shmerapy

tafkid, her role, to help her mother, and she will do the same when she is married with children. Maybe she just needs to talk to her mother at some quiet time, explain how she is feeling, and all will be well. Of course Hashem loves her, and she should do *teshuvah* and never be *mechallel Shabbos* again. This is her *nisayon*, her test, to be the oldest, and Hashem will repay her.

This wonderful *mechaneches* then takes it one step further. She asks around just to make sure everything is all right in this girl's home. Then she hears what wonderful people the parents are, that this girl was always a little bit of a problem, and the rest of the siblings are angels. Nothing is wrong with this girl except that she is a little melodramatic, and her poor parents have their hands full with her.

This misguided teacher is looking at this girl through the lens of her own normalcy. What does she know of mothers with personality disorders and hospitalizations that are kept so secret that not even the children know that their mother disappears every six months not to Florida but to the psychiatric ward? What does this teacher, brought up in her own healthy home, understand of how a father can distort a child's perception to the extent that only the normal one feels abnormal, and is *mechallel Shabbos* as a last desperate plea for help, while the weaker siblings have lost their sense of self, sense of right and wrong, sense of what is normal and what is not?

Therefore, when a husband comes with a *she'eilah*, a halachic question to a Rav, to an exceedingly good-hearted, wholesome community leader, the Rav answers the *she'eilah* without thinking, without saying, "Why are you asking me this *she'eilah*? Where is your wife? I would like to understand where this question is coming from."

And when a child says, "I don't want to go home, ever," the teacher cajoles the child into putting on his coat when she *should* be checking for bruises on his arms or legs, scars on the heart, asking questions and believing every word he says.

And when the child is *mechallel Shabbos*, the teacher should not listen to the content of her words, but to the context. Perhaps the child doesn't know the words of abuse, so she says she has to help too much. Perhaps the child doesn't know the words to say, "I'm afraid," and so she says instead, "I have to dry so many dishes, and it makes me so angry."

When your child tugs at his ears, moans in pain, is sleepless all night long, and is burning up with fever, it is obvious to you that he must have an ear infection. To a professional mental-health therapist, the symptoms of dysfunction are similarly as crystal clear.

It is difficult to take action when the enemy is alien to us.

We don't even know what action to take.

So ask a therapist.

Unfortunately, the therapist knows Evil intimately. They are no strangers to each other. She will introduce the two of you. You will try to understand. You will read some literature. You will learn the enemy. And you will protect the true goodness in our community.

Therapy, Shmerapy

Protecting Those Who Once Protected Us

It is strange to write about a social problem that seems so at odds with our community's values.

Elder abuse?

What on earth is that?

When I was in college studying social work, my first internship was in a home care agency. Most of the agency's clients were people who had been discharged from hospitals and rehabilitation centers and needed the home care service workers to help them transition from hospital/rehab to home. Most of that transition process was setting up nursing care arrangements in the home with a nurse coming in daily or weekly to administer care or bringing in the various therapies like speech, occupational, and physical therapy.

As a social work intern, I only came into the picture when a nurse — usually the first care provider — noticed that the client was lacking basic needs and put in a referral for a social worker to come in, evaluate the situation, and connect the client to necessary community and/or government services.

And most of those people lacking basic needs were the elderly.

Because for the most part, when a child is discharged from a hospital or rehabilitation center, the child is already part of a support system provided by his parents and siblings, school, and Chai Lifeline or other supportive organization. An adult is similarly part of a multifaceted community structure, with his or her own family of origin, spouse and synagogue members offering support.

PART II THE CLIENT

But take an elderly adult, and somehow, the rules completely change.

The elderly person's adult children are often busy with their own lives and either unaware or unable to care for their parent. The spouse of an elderly adult is obviously elderly as well and unable to engage in the physical care of the home and spouse, and this couple, or client, is often isolated from the community, from the block or synagogue who has forgotten them, and from organizations that are more focused on the children and on the adults caring for children.

At my internship, in the capacity of social worker, I was called in to assess the needs of the elderly person, assess what community and government resources were available to help, and put those resources into motion as soon as possible.

I learned a great deal about the resources that can be accessed.

A ramp for a disabled person living in an apartment building, a learning *chavrusa*, a Bubby-sitter in the form a high school volunteer, free home repairs, free furniture, and hot meals delivered daily. Holocaust reparations, free cleaning help, Medicaid, free legal help, free burial, and myriads of other forms of aid to the elderly.

But one of the most powerful tools I learned about was APS — Adult Protective Services.

APS is a program of the HRA, Human Resources Administration, which is more familiar to many as the number to call for Medicaid or Food Stamps.

APS is a state-mandated case management program that arranges for services and support for physically and/or mentally impaired adults who are at risk of harm in their homes. The mission of APS is to enable these people to live independently and safely within their homes and communities.

Look it up and you will find out all about APS.

Anyone can call in a report to APS concerning an adult, much in the same way anyone call in to report a child to Child Protective Services.

And the reasons are often the same.

The adult is being neglected and/or abused by caregivers, whether those caregivers are family members, volunteers, or hired help. The abuse can be verbal or physical, like screaming, hitting, or threatening to withhold food, human company such as grandchildren or guests, or other needs or wants. Neglect can be evident in areas such as personal hygiene, threadbare clothing, moldy food in the fridge, or lack of access to the outside. The adult is living in a home that is unsafe, perhaps unsanitary, as the adult cannot keep the home clean; or, perhaps physically structured so that the elderly person cannot navigate without fear of falling or other injury. Lack of food may be an issue, or there may be financial limitations that make the adult unable to pay heating bills or rent. Somebody may be exploiting the adult financially, suspected of stealing from the adult or coercing the adult to part with her money.

No, you say. This is not happening in my community. This is not happening to our elderly. Not to the sweet Mr. Schwartz in our synagogue; not to the friendly Mrs. Klein on my block.

But yes, it's happening around us.

It's happening in the nicest families.

Sometimes it's happening because the elderly are too proud to tell their children they need help and the adult children may be too wrapped up in their busy lives caring for single and married children, their own grandchildren, and their spouses to realize what is going on. Adult children may be part of the problem as they face frustration and limited finances and crotchety and difficult aging parents, as they struggle to keep all the balls in the air and drop the ones that suddenly become too heavy. Sometimes, there are second marriages and familial conflicts that make it hard for children or others to get involved. Sometimes, these elderly people simply become invisible as their world narrows and they are unable to walk outside as easily as they once did, to shop, to attend synagogue, to engage in volunteer opportunities or jobs; their spouses dead or prey to dementia or Alzheimer's, their reason for getting up in the morning taken away, leaving them floundering in their weakened state, unable to reach out.

Add to the mix a fall, a broken hip, a knee replacement, weeks or months in rehabilitation, where they are forgotten or shunted to the side while they recover, and they return home to a world that has become more alien than they have left.

APS is the number to call when an elderly person is unsafe in his environment or with the people who are supposed to be caring for him. But sometimes, we can be the APS for our own grandparents, parents, neighbors, synagogue-members, or great-aunt whose children live overseas.

There are resources out there for our elderly. And sometimes we are their greatest ones.

Therapy, Shmerapy

The Borderline Mother

This column is about the borderline mother, and I write it to give her child a voice.

I write it so we may hear and do.

I will not talk of the borderline mother who is so dysfunctional that her dress is always disorderly, she is always in conflict with someone or other, she alienates her family and her friends, and often cannot sustain a relationship enough to remain in a marriage or stay employed in a job.

No, I will not talk of her because her children, although they suffer, are often taken under the wing of the community, which recognizes their obvious distress.

Instead, I will speak of the mother with borderline personality disorder (or one with various borderline tendencies on a spectrum that may not reach a full diagnosis) who is a remarkable person. She is charming and intelligent. She is involved in community affairs, often working in the helping professions of teaching or therapy. She holds down a job, runs a beautiful home, and her children often look immaculately groomed and dressed. She talks earnestly to others about the importance of being a good mother. She can be counted on for fun, to hold jobs with responsibility, to discuss issues of concern to the community, and for advice on how to best serve our children.

So, what does it mean to be borderline, you ask?

Someone who has borderline personality disorder lacks the capacity to regulate her emotions. She is a person completely stripped of her skin; her entire being is a huge open wound, so that every human interaction, no matter how benign, feels as painful as touch feels to a burn victim whose entire surface is covered in raw burns and has not yet begun to heal.

A person with borderline personality disorder feels unloved, and although her entire focus is on acquiring love from her husband, friends or children, precisely the opposite occurs as she drives them away with her emotional dysregulation. This bottomless need for love is usually a result of impaired attachment with her own mother who did not have the capacity to love her or to express love to her, or it may stem from childhood trauma.

The borderline mother seeks to control her environment, to acquire the obedience of her children and husband, because she has no other tools by which to make them need her and thus to love her.

She is often capable of masking all this so that she appears to be the model of motherhood, all charity and charm.

She is a person to be pitied, for she is truly a pitiful creature. And if she reaches out for help, we must try to help her with every ounce of our strength.

But the borderline mother rarely recognizes her flaws. So we must reserve and direct our pity instead to her child that must be saved.

For the borderline mother is a frightening thing.

Her rages are terrifying.

She threatens to hurt if her demands are not met. And she often does hurt. With her hands. With objects. With words. She uses awful words, hurtful words, manipulative words, guilt-inducing words.

Children of borderline parents cannot find the words to explain their terror, their distress, their dread. They wake up in fear and return home to fear. They feel unsafe, unprotected, anxious, and depressed. School may be a haven, but they dare not speak.

The borderline mother has perfected guilt to an art. She manipulates her children to take on the burden of feeling a guilt that is almost as paralyzing as the terror.

Sometimes, the distress of some siblings manifests itself in bullying, adding another layer of torment to both the bully and bullied. Especially as the bullied child feels helpless to stop it; feels she has no recourse from her parents or other adults.

Sometimes the borderline mother surprises the child with the most amazing evening out, just the two of them alone, and says the words the child thirsts to hear: "I love you. You are wonderful," and the child thinks that really it is she, the child, who is bad and if she could only try harder to be good, her mother will remain this good mother.

Imagine a child saying, "My mother gets upset when I don't want to finish my chicken."

The teacher or neighbor or grandparent nods sympathetically and says, "Your mother is a wonderful mother. She *does* work hard to make supper every night. You should appreciate her and eat what she gives you." The child is urged, "Make an effort. She cares so much about you!"

The child despairs. Her words are lost in an ocean of unresponsiveness, of obliviousness.

Where is the father, you ask?

He often leaves the house early and comes home late. If the child dares to complain, he says, "Listen to your mother. She is right. She is doing the best she can. You should stop complaining/misbehaving/giving her grief."

And the borderline mother is clever and sly enough that no matter how much she screams or hits or criticizes her children, when her husband is home, she never crosses the line from out-of-control to the pure crazy her children know.

He is afraid too.

He hates conflict.

He pretends he doesn't see; he pretends he doesn't know.

He thinks he is preserving the peace.

Imagine the helpless rage and fears of a child who understands that her mother is so powerful that even her own father is afraid. If her own father cannot protect her, how can she trust any adult? How can she confide in a teacher, her grandparent, the Rebbetzin of her synagogue?

She becomes confused and thinks maybe she truly is as bad as her mother says. Maybe she deserves all the punishment she endures.

Life is a confusing blur of illusion, the blend of her mother's distortions and her father's ghostly presence.

Children of borderline mothers often grow up to perpetuate their mother's legacy — unable to find a sense of self that enables them to form relationships, hold down jobs, or parent their own children. They are bottomless pits of insecurities, fears, and skewed views and attitudes of how the world works.

This column speaks to you: the grandparent, the aunt, the teacher, the principal, the neighbor, the Rav, the Rebbetzin who has some influence over the borderline parent.

Often, if someone speaks up, validating the child's difficult existence, giving the child tools to cope, to change the dynamics of the home; through therapy, through a supportive school or extended family, the family can heal.

Even the borderline mother.

Therapy, Shmerapy

The Borderline Mother Revisited: A Therapist Apologizes

Of all my columns, my article on mothers with borderline personality disorder has evoked the most passionate response. Teenage and adult children of mothers with BPD thanked me for validating their experiences and giving them a voice. Mothers, recognizing for the first time their behavior in terms of a possible BPD diagnosis, reached out for help.

But then I received some more emails from mothers with BPD. And I owe them a public apology — because in my article, I failed to address the BPD mother who is aware of her diagnosis, is in therapy, and is engaging in the most courageous struggle to be the mother her children are lucky to have.

Here are their words:

Your article on mothers with BPD made me feel deeply saddened and misunderstood. I am sure that you do not deal with BPD clients, as you wouldn't betray us so deeply. And you would've come to know us as the beautiful and struggling human beings that we truly are. So now let me tell you who we really are. I was abused throughout my childhood. I was also valedictorian, GO head, and editor of my school newspaper. I was also the girl who my teachers would ask to include and befriend the lonely, shy girls. I had solid, meaningful friendships, and I volunteered for many chessed organizations. I have a huge heart and a dark, twisted, very sad head. When I got married, I was forced to stop hiding and running.

If you were to peg me to one of your two descriptions of BPD mothers, I would be forced into your second category. But I'm not like that at all. I don't manipulate people, and I don't have unreasonable anger. My devoted and loving husband, whom I've been supporting for over ten years in kollel, *is home every evening, and my three kids are well taken care of and well-adjusted kids. They have an open, stable, warm, and loving relationship with my husband and myself.*

There's this mom in my DBT group who put her six-figure career on hold while she takes care of her emotional health. I don't know about you, but I seriously respect that.

In my therapy group, what I hear most is how the parents there want to work hard, take responsibility, and recover in order to be better parents.

What about my BPD, you ask? I sometimes hate myself so much. I feel such emptiness at times that I want to leave everything to escape the pain. I used to be convinced that it was impossible for anyone to love me.

Studies show that 90 percent of people with BPD experienced serious trauma in childhood. In reaction to that trauma, the amygdala [an almond-shaped mass of gray matter inside each cerebral hemisphere involved with the experiencing of emotions] has been activated to the extent that they are constantly in fight or flight mode. Hence, the extreme rage or unregulated responses to perceived threat. But you know what? I'm not looking for validation or sympathy here. My therapy program has taught me to rewire my brain to the extent that I can give myself that validation. While my diagnosis has helped me understand my behaviors and feelings, I take full responsibility for how I react, respond, and, above all, treat others.

・・・

I have been diagnosed with borderline personality disorder and have been seeing a therapist for many years. I am also a brand new mother of all but two-and-a-half weeks at the time of reading your article. Needless to say, the article left me feeling hopeless and panicked. Mindy had painted a horrific future for my brand new baby. I felt sad and guilty about her seemingly inevitable future, until I made the decision that none of what I read was relevant to me.

・・・

Therapy, Shmerapy

BPD does not define me. I am a mother, a wife, a legal professional, a friend, and a daughter. I happen to be struggling with BPD as well. I'm undeservedly blessed because I'm healing. My days of psych wards, paralyzing darkness, and constant instability are, thank G-d, fading.

・・・

So for those of you who read my article in despair because you recognize yourself as the mother with BPD and your future looks bleak, know that this is the second part of the picture. The reality of healing, of help and of hope.

But that healing comes with extreme dedication and the need for support from not only the family, but also of the community. We all need to support the borderline mother because her journey is a difficult journey.

One of the women who wrote to me describes her journey to health consisting of the following: six years of twice weekly therapy. Funds for a nanny. The local *Bikur Cholim* sponsoring weekly suppers and babysitting funds when she was in her therapy program; a two-year commitment to meet twice-weekly for two hours of group therapy and one hour of individual therapy. She writes of the necessity of occasional Shabbos retreats to rest from the strenuous emotional toll of therapy. She speaks of her husband's Rosh Yeshivah, who gave her hours of his time listening and talking; of her husband's Rav, who was supportive and encouraging to her husband, referring them to good therapists.

A mammoth endeavor toward healing.

The gold standard of therapy treatment for clients with BPD is called DBT. Dialectical Behavioral Therapy. The word dialectical means the integration of two diametrically opposed concepts, specifically the paradoxical reality of the need for client change, but the acceptance of the borderline client as she is. In other words, the therapist accepts the client for who she is while insisting that the client must change in order to reach her goal. This therapy encompasses many aspects, with individual and group therapy mandated, as well as phone coaching and skills. There are four specific DBT skills that are taught: mindfulness and distress tolerance — both of which focus on *acceptance* of what is — and interpersonal effectiveness and emotional regulation — which are designed to *change* the nature of interpersonal relationships and emotions.

But not all clients with BPD need such extensive treatment because there is a continuum of borderline along a spectrum of various degrees of severity.

Once, BPD was considered a therapist's nightmare; today there are statistically proven successful treatments.

So I apologize once more to those mothers with BPD who are not the mothers of my previous article — because they are heroically taking steps to heal. And they give hope to not only the other BPD parents who read my article and reached out for help, but for all of us, that if we care enough about our children, we can be the mothers we want to be.

Therapy, Shmerapy

Deprived Of Touch, We Lose Our Touch

When a set of twins were born prematurely and were hooked up to every wire and tube necessary to keep them alive, this was the doctor's stringent order to their mother: "You must touch them every single day."

So the mother watched in horror as every lifesaving tube and wire was unhooked, but, as the nurses emphatically explained as they gently placed her tiny, fragile twins into her arms, "Your children need your touch to survive as urgently as those tubes and wires."

I know this story is true because I have met the twins, now grown up, married with children, miracles who once weighed two pounds each.

Here is the story I hear all the time from my clients: "I was never touched as a child. I was never told, 'I love you.'"

"Really?" I ask.

"Really," they answer.

Then my clients think about it.

"Oh, maybe when I was a baby. Because I see how my mother hugs the baby. I see how she hugs the grandchildren. But I don't remember any of it."

"Do you think you mother doesn't love you?" I ask.

"She loves me," they sometimes concede. "But I only *know* it. I don't *feel* it."

The desire to be held, to be touched, to be loved by a mother is so strong, that no other touch can ever suffice, even when these clients go on to hug and kiss and whisper a hundred I-love-you's into the ears of their many children and grandchildren.

Did you ever hear about Harlow?

Ever heard about his monkeys?

Fascinating story, so I gotta tell you about it.

Dr. Harry F. Harlow was an American psychologist whose studies and experiments with monkeys have given us incredible information about how physical demonstrations of love affect a child's ability or impaired ability to form relationships throughout life with significant others such as spouses, children, or non-family members.

As social relationships are the foundation of all of human experiences, the implications of his findings are powerful statements of how we must parent our children or risk devastating consequences.

In one experiment, he separated newly born monkeys and created wire figures that could give milk. He also created figures that did not give milk but were draped in cloth instead of wire. Although the monkeys went to the wire mothers for milk, most of their time otherwise was spent clinging to the cloth mothers, demonstrating how the monkeys valued the cloth mother in its ability to give physical affection, so to speak, more than the wire mother which dispensed life-giving food. Attachment is more dependent on physical affection than being fed.

Following these maternal-deprived baby monkeys into adulthood showed striking results. Negative traits like aggressiveness, clinginess, and a tendency towards social isolation, as well as neglect or even abuse of offspring, were some observations.

Psychology points to the exact same results in human babies starved for physical attention and love.

It explains why babies left in orphanages, despite being adequately fed and cleaned, simply died for lack of love. *Failure to thrive* was the term coined by research scientists who studied this phenomenon, leading to revolutionary changes in orphanages, with caregivers directed to give physical touch along with bottles.

Many studies try to understand the correlation between touch and physical and emotional health. One explanation is that affectionate touch lowers an individual's stress and anxiety levels. Touch deprivation raises stress levels; increased production of stress hormones like cortisol and norepinephrine is then found in the blood. Chronically high levels of cortisol prevent normal brain tissue development in children and damage existing brain tissue, especially the hippocampus. The hippocampus is involved in memory and learning, explaining why children deprived of touch have, statistically, more learning difficulties.

Affectionate touch activates different hormones than stress does, eventually changing an individual's brain chemistry.

Children who lack affectionate touch and experience chronic stress as a result have weakened immune systems. This accounts for the poor health and abnormal growth found in children deprived of touch.

Luckily, we are not monkeys and children deprived of touch can still be healthy adults. We call them "resilient."

And many of these studies point to the ability of these resilient children to reach out to others who become the mother figures their own mother cannot be.

In contrast to the effects of touch deprivation, children exposed regularly to affectionate touch have an enhanced ability to problem-solve, recover from illness more rapidly, suffer less anxiety, show lower propensity for cardiovascular disease as adults, and have higher tolerance for emotional and physical pain.

They are more confident and social; they have the capacity to form relationships easily and comfortably, to go on to marry and form good relationships with their spouses, and later to be affectionate and attentive parents to their own children. Even learning is easier for these children, making their school years more enjoyable and productive.

Often, adults who have been deprived of physical affection as children may look successful, act successful, exude success — but inside there is a hole so vast, so deep, so terrible, that secretly they struggle with anxiety, depression, guilt, and anger.

The irony is that if these mothers were confronted, they would be devastated. Because they love their children with such a fierce passion that there isn't a burning building too hot they would not enter to save their child.

These mothers would say, "What did I know of hugging? My mother never hugged me, and I turned out fine."

Maybe.

Maybe not.

I watch many people in my community, how the babies are kissed and hugged non-stop and then those same exhibitions of affections dry up and are only available for the next little one, as if touch, as if kisses and hugs, are a limited commodity.

I can't give you the answers of why this happens. But I do know that a mother needs to show the love she has for her children with touch. Because she *has* the love to give. I know that. Her children know that. But the *knowledge* of the love is simply *not good enough*. Only a hug will do.

Try it. Even now. Stroke your child's hair, pat a shoulder or cheek. Give a hug, plant a kiss. Your kid will squirm, will protest, "Ma-a-a!" But secretly your child will enjoy it.

And so will you.

Part III
The Therapist and Client

I need you! I need to be loved!

The third level of the pyramid, once survival and safety are in place, is the urgent need for love and belonging. This need manifests in many ways. How we long to belong to our family, to our community, to our religion. We work towards belonging to our chosen profession, to peers of our choosing, to bungalow colonies and the little cliques that congregate either in shul or outside waiting together for the school buses. We cannot live in isolation. We starve for human companionship, for our parents to love us, for our siblings, friends, and colleagues to value us.

I remember the words of one of my supervisors, a gentile woman with tremendous respect for the diverse cultures that she saw in her office from clients or supervisees.

"It's the humanness in all of us that transcends all else,
that is important to relationships;
relationships build bridges between people
and make a difference in our lives."

And the beautiful poetry of a client who had converted to Judaism, expressing her appreciation for a culture she worked hard to join.

"The non-Jewish experience is like a fruit,
an orange.
It's delicious —
you can bite right into it
and it's rich with flavor and taste.
Maybe to eat it,
you need to peel the outer cover,
but it's right there to experience.

Therapy, Shmerapy

The Jewish experience is like an onion.
There are layers and layers of it.
And you can't just bite into it.
You need to dice it, fry it, sauté it...
but imagine life without onions!
It's a part of everything...
I am awed by the Orthodox Jewish lifestyle,
the casualness of leading a lifestyle
drenched
in 5,000 years of Judaism."

PART III THE THERAPIST AND CLIENT

Bound to Have Boundaries

Listen to me.

You may find yourself in this scenario.

For months you have been miserable. Maybe years. You have spoken to friends, confided in mentors, consulted with rabbis, and vented to sisters. But you just didn't feel better. So you let your husband, your friend, your **rav**, or even your own dear self convince you to try therapy.

And, it must be a coincidence, but within a few weeks of beginning therapy, you actually start to feel better. Like I said, a coincidence. Probably nothing at all to do with therapy, but fine, you'll continue with therapy... just in case it's actually therapy that's making you feel better...

But then therapy starts bugging you. Not only is therapy starting to bug you, the therapist is beginning to bug you, too.

You feel stupid paying her just to talk to her. I mean, can't you just talk to your sister?

And you hate the way it's exactly fifty minutes a session, and as soon as that clock ticks and tocks onto the fiftieth minute of the hour, your therapist tells you that time is up. Like, why can't she just let it be an hour? What's an extra ten minutes?

And it annoys you that you can't just call your therapist any old time you want. I mean, you could, but it feels weird because you usually pay her, so you feel strange if you call. And anyway, what exactly are you calling about? It's not like you can schmooze with your therapist. She's not your friend or anything.

You are not even sure **what** she is. Okay, she's a therapist. But what does that mean? And what's with all these boundaries on how long your sessions are and when you can call her?

If you are in therapy, these questions sound familiar. Even if you are not in therapy, you may have been wondering about the same things. Or if someone you know or love is in therapy, you may not understand these boundaries, and would like to understand so you can be more supportive.

Therapy is very different from any other relationship, even other helping relationships, because of its set of boundaries. These boundaries are about paying the therapist for each session. It's about how long each session is, how to manage out-of-session contact between therapist and client, and the consistency of appointments. Boundaries monitor the therapist's self-disclosure and maintain confidentiality. There may be other boundaries, but these are the main ones I will explore in this column.

Therapy works to relieve the person's symptoms that bring him into therapy to begin with, in ways that talking to a friend, sibling, or **Rav** cannot. It's because of the boundaries of the therapy experience, so different from the boundaries in a friendship, within family, or as a constituent of a **Rav**, that a person finally finds relief from the burden of pain, anxiety, or depression they have carried for months or sometimes, years.

If a therapist would not charge money, would not abide by the constraints of the therapy hour and the need to identify boundaries of contact outside sessions, and maintain confidentiality, then the therapist would be the same as the other helpers who were **not** successful in helping you.

The therapy hour is an experience, the effect of which spreads over the week. It is not isolated to the single fifty minutes in which the client and therapist meet. It creates a disequiblium in the client so that positive change is forced to occur.

Everything that happens in the therapy room is significant.

And that is why the therapeutic boundaries are so crucial. They keep

PART III THE THERAPIST AND CLIENT

the client safe while therapy does its work.

A therapist who keeps a client overtime past the session, or cannot create/maintain appropriate boundaries with regard to out-of-session contact may be sending messages like, **Your problems are so terrible, I must help you more**, or **Only I can help you, so I will give you more time**, or **Your problems are so huge, you can't possibly manage them by yourself, so I need to give you more time.**

Boundaries of space and time and payment convey a powerful and positive message: **You are capable of doing the work you need to do to feel better, and I am only a temporary facilitator.**

It would be inappropriate in most cases for a therapist to meet a client in any other venue but the therapy room, except where therapy is otherwise established (i.e. if a client is anorexic, therapy may take place in restaurants or other such places). A therapist would not invite a client to her home, attend her **simchos**, or spend an inordinate amount of hours together, even if there is payment for those hours. A therapist's self disclosure is generally inappropriate. When a therapist self-discloses, the information being disclosed must be carefully judged and found to be therapeutically necessary or sound. It can **never** be for the therapist's aggrandizement or personal needs.

When a client pays a therapist, it forces the two to acknowledge that even though the therapist has chosen to go into this field from a desire to help, it is still a job, and it is the responsibility of the therapist to do her job. If the job is not being done satisfactorily, there must be constant assessment of why, and a revision of how the client's needs would best be met. There are treatment goals and objectives; this is not simply two friends, or a mentor and disciple, meeting once a week to talk. Payment makes that very clear. Foregoing payment blurs this understanding of the roles of client and therapist.

As a therapist, I know that a client struggles with her feelings of weirdness that she must pay to talk to someone when she can talk to her friends for free. So when a client shows discomfort, resistance, or anger at the reality of this and other therapeutic boundaries, I find it important to acknowledge them, even if the client is unable to process the reasons why they exist.

Of course, therapists are human (surprise, surprise!), and sometimes we make mistakes with boundaries. And sometimes in our humanness, we also sometimes break boundaries. And yes, we will go over the fifty minutes, and we will take a reduced rate, and we will accept a call in between the client's sessions, and we will accidentally self-disclose.

If you want to know the truth, here it is: Sometimes we are really enjoying your company and wish we can spend another hour with you, and sometimes we wish we can see you for free, and sometimes we wish we can self-disclose and let you know how we really understand your pain because we have been there, too.

But because we care, the greatest gift we can give you is to keep you safe within the therapeutic boundaries so that in time, you will no longer need us.

Following Up On "Bound to Have Boundaries"

This article was written in response to Bound to Have Boundaries after being inundated with letters from readers of *Binah Magazine*. The letter below and my response deals with my readers' concerns that boundaries between a therapist and client can also be a double-edged sword and serve as an impediment to the client.

Dear Editor,
This is the first time in my life I have written a letter to the editor, although I am an avid reader, especially of *Binah*. I am writing regarding Mrs. Mindy Blumenfeld's recent article, "Bound to have Boundaries." I enjoy Mrs. Blumenfeld's column, especially as I have been in therapy myself. I would like to voice some of my questions/concerns as someone on the other side of the "therapy desk."

Mrs. Blumenfeld states that boundaries "keep the client safe while therapy does its work." I am a great fan of boundaries. I believe that if boundaries weren't set, clients would abuse the therapists' time, become dependent on their therapists, and the relationship would be dysfunctional and ineffective. And yet at the same time, I believe that the boundaries must be set with good sense and compassion.

From my experience, as well as that of many others I know, it is not at all assured that within a few weeks of starting therapy the client will feel better, as the articles suggests. I would like to explain a bit of what the client experiences, which, although every experience is unique, I'm sure many others can identify with.

Therapy, Shmerapy

The client enters the therapist's office with a mixture of terror and hope, looking to find some relief from her debilitating pain. The first session may make her feel better, as she feels she has finally found someone who really listens to her and can understand her. Trouble may develop throughout the next few sessions, and may last for weeks or months, as the therapist encourages the client to open up. The client digs deep down and brings her pain into the open. As the session goes on, many difficult emotions may come to the fore: shame, sadness, anger, feelings of rejection, self-loathing, weariness, and others, depending on the individual. This emotion digging is a vital part of the process, as suppressed feelings cause a lot of damage.

But the client may be in midsentence when the fifty or so minutes are up. She then leaves for home. When she returns to her regular life as a student, or a mother, or a wife, or an employee, or some combination of the above, something has changed within her. Painful emotions that may have been suppressed until now are roiling under the surface. The client might find herself functioning even less effectively than usual, and may be more angry, sad, or withdrawn. If difficult memories have been discussed, she may have nightmares. On top of the difficulties that brought her to therapy, she needs to cope with the difficult emotions that the therapy sessions have raised.

Due to the long journey the client still has to take, she has not yet had a chance to learn all the skills she needs to deal with these difficult emotions. She is now in a quandary. She cannot contact her therapist due to professional boundaries.

This all-too-real scenario leaves many clients in a catch-22 situation. We believe therapy will eventually help us. We want to stand on our own two feet and do our own work. Yet, upon starting therapy, our situation may initially get worse. It is not enough to assure us that eventually we will feel better. Our families might be counting on us. We can't take a break from school or work for the next few months until we feel better. And worst of all, therapy might bring up so much pain that we might need some first-aid to deal with it. But because our therapist is only accessible during session time, we might feel that we are going through this alone with no one to turn to.

I do not know how to address this problem. I think that this is something that we as a community must think long and hard about. We can't just assume that everything is fine because "she is going for therapy." The client may need much more help and support precisely because of that.

There might even be a more difficult development, namely, if the therapist and client aren't a good match, or the client's trust has been violated in some way. Believe me, this happens more than one might think. Then the client needs to deal with the agony of sharing her deepest feelings with someone, believing that she would be helped that way, and facing the disappointment and the arduous process of starting all over again.

My question for therapist is this: Are boundaries set in stone? Shouldn't a therapist be available, not on a steady basis, but at a time when a client is going through a crisis for which she does not have the skills to cope? And if the therapist cannot violate the boundaries, is there someone else the client can turn to? Should every client, perhaps, be assigned a mentor of sorts to help her through the process? I would really appreciate if Mrs. Blumenfeld can answer some of my questions.

There are several other points I'd like to make about the boundaries mentioned. I understand the need for a therapist not to share her personal life with the client. Frankly, most clients aren't interested in their therapist's story, and are only there to get help.

However, remaining too aloof and refraining from making any small talk, such as, "Oh, I love bagels too!" can inhibit the client from sharing information. Everybody likes to feel that they're talking to a caring human being, not a robot, especially when they're baring their soul.

There is also a very difficult question that we often ask ourselves: "Does my therapist *care*?" In almost any profession, a person will have to prove themselves and their dedication to their jobs. In the human relations field, a person might also have to prove that she cares for her clients in order to establish a relationship of trust.

In the medical field, or the educational field, if a client feels that she isn't getting the required care or there is a problem with the care, there is usually a higher authority to whom to bring complaints. In therapy, a client can have a hard time distinguishing if the therapist is trying to get away with doing the minimum or even less, or if the therapist is truly doing the best she can and cares about succeeding.

For one, most clients don't know a lot about what therapy is supposed to be like. The therapist may encourage the client to talk and spend time listening. However, after many weeks the client feels that she has made no improvement. The therapist may tell her that she just needs to talk more. The client is confused: Is the therapist right? Shouldn't she try a different angle or spend more time teaching coping skills? Is the therapist spending time doing research, thinking of different approaches, or is she resting on her laurels? Is there any incentive for her to do more or try harder, or is she content to let things slide as the client will just take her word on everything? And last but not least, is there anyone the client can approach with her questions?

I don't mean to imply that all therapists aren't doing their best. Unfortunately, I am basing my comments on real life experiences of myself and others. One therapist cut my session short while taking the full fee, ironically, because she had a meeting with her supervisor! I realized that while she did have who to ask for advice, I had no one to turn to with my complaint, as I had no clue that she believed that just by feeling safe to talk to her about anything I would get better. This may work for some, but I definitely was disappointed. I can't imagine that just talking would help people with issues that, in order to heal from them, require the acquisition of new skills or a more directed kind of therapy. This therapist said she would be fine if I only talked about what I had for breakfast! If a client with serious issues chooses to do just that, I wondered, will she get better? Is this therapist right, ineffective, or does she just not care?

Although I did find a therapist in the end with whom I had a long-term relationship, and who has helped me tremendously, I discontinued seeing her several years ago for various reasons. I am now at a stage where I am thinking about continuing with therapy. I want a therapist who will treat me as an intelligent person who happens to be going through a hard time. I do not want to fall apart during therapy and not have who to reach out to. I do not want to use a therapist who uses boundaries as an excuse to slack off. I would love for there to be a knowledgeable person for me to discus my questions/concerns about the direction the therapy is taking.

I think it is also important that *frum* publications don't tout therapy as a magic cure, but instead as a long, arduous journey to self-fulfillment. I think there also needs to be some acknowledgment that not everyone with a license is an effective therapist for everyone. I would also love to hear it acknowledged that a client had a right to ask questions and have a say in the course of her treatment, while of course doing her best to get better.

With the above said, I absolutely encourage everyone in need of help to go for therapy. The right therapist can make a huge difference in your life, as it did in mine. I just think it would be very helpful to portray a realistic picture of therapy and work as a community to straighten the kinks in the system.

Sincerely yours,
Name withheld

My response:

Are Boundaries Backfiring?

If I would have known what an outpouring of mail and phone calls my article "Bound to Have Boundaries" would generate, I would have hired a secretary!

I didn't. Instead, I read through all the mail on my own, took careful notes, and now write this follow up in response to all my eloquent writers whose letters raised so many questions focusing on nuanced issues of boundaries between client and therapist.

I love the way the letter writer wrote, "I believe that boundaries, as with all other concepts, must be set with good sense and compassion." And I am glad that we share that sentiment.

Some of my readers understood that having boundaries means to strictly adhere to contact only within sessions. Not at all. My clients have my email address and my cell phone number. They can call, email, or text. But there is no violation of boundaries when they do so because these in-between-session contacts are already embedded in the therapeutic structure. I will clearly delineate these boundaries by saying something like, "If you need to, call and leave a message. I will call you back when I have free time, although it may not be for a few hours." I may say, "If you text me, I can answer quickly, but I do not do text conversations other than to set up or change appointments." I will encourage journaling throughout the week and say, "Email me your journals so I can read/print it out before you come."

Sometimes, when I know a person needs more frequent contact than I have time to give, I will say, "Call and leave a message. I won't answer it, but you will know that I have heard you." Often that knowledge is enough.

And I would follow up that statement with, "And if you really need to reach out, tell me that specifically in your message so I can call you back." Often that knowledge of my availability is enough to hold a client in-between sessions. Because if leaving a message or email is not enough, a client can help me know what she needs and together we can build a new structure that will have its own set of boundaries.

So it's not that therapy must be rigid; not at all. Each therapeutic experience and relationship is unique. The needs of each client are unique. We create a new form or style of therapy for each client. What remains the same is the need to build in boundaries within the individual structures.

PART III THE THERAPIST AND CLIENT

If a client is struggling with maintaining boundaries (she needs to call endlessly, texts endlessly, checks out where the therapist lives), then that is another element that needs to be addressed during therapy; grist for the mill, as Dr. Irwin Yalom calls it. Nothing more or less. But if a therapist cannot maintain the boundaries, then the structure and safety for the client has been compromised.

Therapy is sometimes an arduous journey to self-fulfillment; however, it should not be a journey with no end. It has a beginning, a middle, and an end, a structure that a therapist should be able to identify and share with her client. The magic in therapy is that it allows a person to achieve the goals for which they entered therapy, not that it is in and of itself magical or easy as magic. Boundaries help define the limited nature of this relationship so that therapy itself is limited to goal-setting and achieving, not becoming and it-feels-good-but-I'm-really-not-accomplishing-anything type of relationship.

Therapist self-disclosure seems to have generated much controversy among my readers.

Allow me to clarify. There a few types of self-disclosure: Disclosure about a therapist's training and background relevant to practice, disclosure about a therapist's life outside of the therapy room, and disclosure in the here-and-now of the therapeutic session.

A rule of thumb is that a client has every right to request information about the therapist's training, theoretical orientation, and method of doing therapy, and the client can expect a clear answer about anything related to those. I personally feel that a client could ask a therapist who her supervisor is, with which rav she is *sho'el eitzah*, and the contact information of the licensing board to which she is answerable in case of questionable practice. Every licensed therapist is under the jurisdiction of a licensing board to which clients can formally lodge complaints should a therapist act unethically.

A client should be able to ask how a therapist practices and continue to demand answers throughout therapy. The therapist should absolutely be able to answer a client's questions intelligently. Not just say, "The more you talk, the better you will feel." She should be able to clearly explain her theoretical orientation, modalities, and interventions she uses, and explain the rationale behind her methods. Although therapy may look like a just talk kind of thing, there are many ways to practice therapy responsibly using evidence-based techniques and theories.

A client can ask a therapist any question she so pleases about the therapist's private life, because the therapy room is a place for the client to say whatever she wants. Nothing is forbidden.

It is the therapist's prerogative to either answer or to decline answering. My personal preference about answering client's questions is to usually answer if I don't mind doing so, and then follow up either then, or file it away for a different time to explore the client's motivation and need to ask. If I don't want to answer a question, either because I feel it is not appropriate to reveal or because it would not be helpful to the client, I will be honest with my reasons for withholding.

When I will self-disclose without the client's request to do so, I will do it usually for the one simple reason. To break the client's isolation. I, too, was lousy at math in high school, even almost failing geometry in tenth grade, I tell some of my teen clients.

I too, I may tell adult clients, struggled with toilet training my child.

I will usually choose self-disclosure that is not a present issue for me, as I do not want to burden my clients with my troubles. That would be unfair to them and a terrible breach of boundaries.

Sometimes, my self-disclosure is simply to reveal myself as human, to form a connection to a person who badly needs to feel the caring of another human beside her who is not so different in many ways. So yes, I may say that I love writing or vanilla ice cream with colorful sprinkles, same as they do. Or explain that I must reschedule an appointment not because their lives and problems are inconsequential or inconvenient to me, but because I must attend my child's PTA conference that evening.

I use my judgment when I feel it would be beneficial to give my client a reason for my rescheduling and when it is simply okay to just say, "I need to reschedule. When would be another good time for you?"

But simply to engage in small talk about myself? No. Absolutely not.

Everything that takes place in the therapy hour must be purposeful. So if a client needs small talk to create an opening to talk about the big stuff, the small talk must be purposeful and laden with meaning as well. Self-disclosure as a means of small talk is unacceptable, in my opinion.

The last type of self-disclosure is one I use when I work in the here-and-now of the therapy session. It's letting the client know what is happening in the therapy room with me as I feel it and see it, such as what I am thinking or feeling in response to what is happening between us. It's something like, "I feel that you are disappointed in me somehow. Maybe it's because you feel I am not doing a good enough job in helping your anxiety go away."

Such self-disclosure usually allows the client to relax, knowing that his thoughts are not forbidden, and it lets them know that it's okay to criticize me, to let me know what is not working for her and what she needs from me to get better.

Sometimes I will say, "It feels to me that it's hard for you to like me very much. And instead, you get angry in this room. Like you did right now, when you turned your face away from me as you spoke."

Some clients may think that if a therapist stays overtime in session, is available at all times, lets the client call indiscriminately, and engages in conversation about her family, her troubles, or her interests, it is a sign of her caring.

I would say unequivocally these boundary violations that are not within the context of anything I have written in this article are more a sign of the therapist's own issues, incompetence, and failure to care.

When a therapist cares about her client, the client knows. And if the client does not know, chances are that part of the client's reasons for coming into therapy is the difficulties she is experiencing in interpersonal relationships and other boundary violations in his life outside the therapy walls.

When boundaries are violated, a client usually can feel something is wrong. But the love-like relationship is so strong, it's hard to break out of that cycle.

The greatest caring a therapist can demonstrate is how to protect one's boundaries so that true interpersonal relationships can exist and flourish. Including the therapeutic one.

Hoopla About the Hug

Okay, so you want to know what's with the hug.

The hug?

Yep, the hug.

The hug most clients want from their therapists, whether or not they ask for it.

Oh, *that* hug.

It's a taboo subject, you know. It's not something I would ask another therapist. Like, "Do you hug your clients?" because we are not supposed to be hugging clients. That's all in the literature. Do the research and try to find stuff on therapists hugging clients. It's like trying to find the winning lottery ticket number. It's that hard to find a straight answer.

If any of my clients are reading this (and yes, I know quite a few of you read my columns, so know that I am talking straight to you!), they probably are really curious about my answer. "So, does Mindy hug her clients? Hey, has somebody been getting hugs and it wasn't *me*?"

As an object relations/attachment therapist, I believe that the relationship between client and therapist is crucial to therapy in order to repair damage done in primary relationships that are interfering in present functioning; so this hugging question becomes significant. It's the great pink elephant in the therapy room, and it's just a matter of time before it surfaces.

Before I go further, I will explain a very important word in therapy-language. It's called *transference*. In simple English, it is when people transfer their feelings — and reactions — onto people in their present life;

feelings that really have their roots in prior relationships and often make no sense in the present situation.

Let me explain because we do it all the time so you will catch on pretty quickly.

Let's say you are working at a job as a secretary. And a new workmate says in a friendly manner, "Do you mind bringing me back a hot chocolate when you go out for your lunch break?" and suddenly you are gripped with this very nasty feeling and you think to yourself, *Who does she think she is, asking me to get her stuff that she can do by herself? I hate being used, and I bet she won't pay me back and I'm not going to act petty by asking her for that dollar! She has such nerve asking me!*

In all probability, the workmate is a perfectly ordinary person — as are you — who has no ulterior motives to use you or to steal your money or time, and will very gladly return the favor for you a different time. However, what has kicked in here is transference! You may have had an elementary school friend, neighbor, cousin, or older sister with whom you had such relationship. Someone who used to ask you for favors and never repay them, take advantage of you, or make you feel used. And now, when your workmate innocently enacted a similar behavior, it triggered a response based on old relationships.

To bring this closer to home, we do this all the time with our spouses and children without realizing it. We snap at our husband when he offers to bathe the baby, and we accuse him of thinking we aren't good mothers, when in reality, he is only trying to help and we have transferred onto him a pattern of an old relationship in which our fathers, teachers, or older brothers have conveyed that message in our childhood with a similar behavior. Like when your older brother said, "Let me hang up the painting," and implicit in his words was that you were a *shlemazel* who couldn't get anything done, or done right.

In steps the therapist. After the first few sessions of therapy, the transference kicks in big time. If the therapist didn't greet you with her usual warmth, you transfer your feelings of anger at your mother over

PART III THE THERAPIST AND CLIENT

to her and accuse her of not caring. If she must cancel an appointment, you accuse her (either verbally or in your heart) of not being reliable, consistent, or honest, reminiscent of your father, your teacher, or your counselor who hurt you.

And for some clients, intense feelings of love toward the therapist is often another piece of the transference. It is usually the painful love the client feels for his parent with whom he has a complicated relationship.

These loving feelings are so strong that they don't even make sense in any other context other than the transference. This transference is important, and part of the healing, make no mistake. But within this therapeutic setting, there are strong feelings of wanting to be held by the therapist, rocked, and hugged.

And when these feeling arise from the transference, it would often be harmful for the therapy, even unethical, for a therapist to hug a client.

Gila Manolson, in her beautiful book, *The Magic Touch*, writes about the power of physical touch, that it can only come after a true emotional relationship or else it will create a glue that binds two unrelated objects together (as in two people who are really not connected and therefore should not marry). So too, a hug would create a bond for the client that has nothing to do with the therapist and put up a wall, a cocoon, that would obstruct work on the real relationship issues in the client's world that need mending.

While a therapist-client relationship *is* most assuredly a real relationship, the real part of it is not the intense loving feelings a client has for the therapist that demands a hug or to be held.

So no, as a rule, I do not hug clients.

It would *not* be appropriate for a therapist to initiate a hug. But it would be okay if a client asks for a hug as a way of saying goodbye and thank you at the termination of a successful therapy. And it would be okay if a client asks for a hug when some terrible —or wonderful — event occurs that is out of the therapy structure (she loses her grandmother, she gets engaged...). And it would be okay to touch a client if a client is elderly and needs help putting on a coat. **It may be okay when the hug is not associated with the transference but takes place in the *real* relationship of the therapeutic environment.**

It doesn't mean a therapist *will* hug if a client asks under those circumstances because therapists still have their own personal boundaries concerning space and touch, but rather that touch may be considered appropriate.

Here's the stuff I have in my office that can symbolically give my clients the touch, hug, and holding they crave.

I have heart stickers they can take, or I can be asked to give. I have colored stones that say things on them like *courage, one day at a time, hope,* and *consider yourself hugged;* and these stones fit in the palm of the hand comfortably all through the session and are then returned to the little glass dish when the session is over, to be re-used a different time, or by a different client. I have a red blanket that can be drawn around the shoulders in a tight embrace, and I have pillows that can be squeezed or hugged.

And sometimes, when my client asks for a hug, I will say, "Let this room hold you."

PART III THE THERAPIST AND CLIENT

Therapist, What Do You See When I Sit in Your Office?

"What do you think of us?" a reader asks me in an email. *"I would love to read about how you and other therapists view us, your clients. Yes, we have issues to work on. Yes, we have waited too long to begin this journey. True, we are a work in progress. But, honestly, my friends and I (who are seeing therapists for different reasons) are amazing women! How do you see us?"*

I was intrigued by this question and sent it out to two groups. Both of these groups are comprised of mental health professionals, many of them therapists for the *frum* communities in the USA, Israel, and around the world. I received many responses.

This is what your therapist thinks of you:

"There is a profound appreciation for the richness of what happens between therapist and patient. I also become aware of my deep feeling of gratitude for what I *get* in the process of 'giving': my appreciation for being able to be an instrument of healing and my awe in the face of often unimaginable pain and courage."

"I just completed my first Ironman triathlon (a 3.86 km swim, a 180.25 km bike ride followed by a 42.2 km run; basically 140.6 miles in one day). Healing from trauma is way harder than this Ironman ever will be."

"My clients show up week after week, enduring, processing, and managing unbelievable pain and suffering with a tenacity that is astounding. They work hard at healing; they are brave, bright, inspiring, amazing humans. They show me and all of us the best of human behavior. They fight tooth and nail, every day, to be okay, and most of them, in the end, find joy. Most of them learn peace, love, and a solid sense of self."

"I am gifted to know them; I am lucky to witness their recovery. They shine brighter than most. I see a beauty in them when they first show up; getting to witness the process where they learn of that beauty themselves, especially after all of the harm, is simply magical."

"I view my clients as people with the same emotions, capabilities, situations, experiences that people in my own life may have. I teach them, but they are my greatest teachers."

"[I view my clients no different than I view others in my life,] with capabilities and limitations. I realize that people can be stuck, just like [I and] the people in my life can be stuck. If I can be patient with my patients, I can learn to be patient with my family, friends, employees and co-workers… My clinical director stated that to avoid burnout you must be interested in your clients. It's very true. And I am."

"I view my clients as brave individuals who have the courage to reach out and ask for help to make their lives and the lives of those they love better."

"[I see] each one as individual, and I pray [I will be the one] to help facilitate healing and personal growth. [There is] a unique bond that develops when people share themselves [as it inevitably happens in our therapeutic alliance]."

"I often wish my clients knew in what high regard I hold them from our first meeting. Each new person who is brave enough to face themselves in the presence of another person whom they have just met gains my immediate respect. The fact that they are in my office means that whatever their background — from criminal to addict to a stressed wife or anxious teen — they are hurting inside, want something better; and they deserve to feel peaceful, safe, and comfortable in their own skin. It is an honor to assist them to discover, sometimes for the first time in their lives, the beauty of their true essence. To awaken the confident, maybe playful, but always kind and gentle soul within each client is a privilege that allows me to have a continual curiosity about their life experiences,

PART III THE THERAPIST AND CLIENT

what shaped them into who they are today and how we can together get them where they want to go. I notice that I usually expect the best from them since I get to see a lot of their 'good side,' which has a positive effect on us both!"

"How do I view my clients? From 360 degrees. Seeking the child within. Using all my senses. With curiosity. With my third ear. Not as my friend, sister, spouse or child, but as that wonderfully unique person — 'my client.' Very humbling."

"My background is in theater. I was an actress for 25 years before I began my career as a therapist, which I have been in for the last 20 years. As an actress, I was taught, and I believe, that you cannot play a character successfully unless you can find a way to love that character. I fully believe the same thing working with my clients, that I cannot work with them successfully unless I can find a way to love them. And I do love and care deeply about my clients."

These beautiful responses eloquently echo how I would respond to my reader's question. I remember sitting with a client who was undergoing tremendous challenges. Despite it all, she had a wonderful smile, kept her sense of humor, worked hard as a mother, and always walked in with style and poise, her makeup artfully applied. Towards the end of the session, without any forethought, I blurted, "You have no idea how much I respect you!" And even when I don't express it that openly, my admiration is always in the room. I hope my clients feel it as strongly as I do.

As many therapists responded, as human beings we all have the innate need to connect to another person, and a therapist is often the first such connection. We are honored to be that person in which healing — through connection — can begin to occur. That we become the catalyst, the messenger, Hashem's *shaliach*, for a client's journey to wholeness.

Surprisingly, I learned one more thing from the responses I received (because some annoyed me tremendously!): One of the surest ways to know if a therapist is a good fit for you is to ask him or her this question. A therapist who cannot answer this seemingly innocuous question,

Therapy, Shmerapy

or a therapist whose answer turns you off (which may be different for individuals!) is a therapist who is not right for you.

So thank you, dear Reader-from-Brooklyn, for your fabulous, thought-provoking question!

Therapy Is Not Helping, Part 1

I love this one.

I have a mother (or wife or husband or even teenager) sitting in my office. And she clearly needs individual counseling. But when I encourage her to seek therapy for herself while I work with her teen (or husband or mother or whoever), she says, "Therapy doesn't work. Therapy doesn't help." And yet, this same mother tells me, "I can't believe how my Chaim/Suri/Sprintzy/Yanky/Ahuva has changed since beginning therapy!" She refuses to hear the ridiculousness of her statement denying the efficacy of therapy for herself and singing its virtues for her daughter.

I shrug my shoulders and sigh.

Because I hear other stuff. You know how it is. I am sitting at the pool minding my own business when people assume I represent all Social Workers Around America and tell me things like, "I heard So-and-So paid a ton of money for marriage counseling and they still have a lousy marriage." Or, "My neighbor went to top therapist Whatsisname with her son, and he still does XYZ, driving his mother crazy!" Or, "I went to a therapist for a year, and it was very nice, but really, she didn't help me at all."

Groan. I am relaxing with my book — do you mind?

I'm only joking. My book can wait (*Stop Obsessing*, if you must know).

So what's the deal with therapy? How do I know if it's helping me or I am just wasting my time?

The best way to know if therapy is helping you is if your therapist is paying off his son's wedding with your fees. Just kidding! I said, just kidding!

In order to know if therapy is helping, it's important to know a few things. Who is the client? What does the client want to accomplish? Are the goals reasonable? Does the client have the tools to reach those goals? What are the obstacles to achieving those goals?

A parent brings a teenager into therapy and orders me to, "Fix him!" My question is, "Who is the client here? Is it the teenager or the mother?" It sounds like a silly question, right? Because if the son is acting out at school, being rude and disrespectful, accessing technology despite clear prohibitions against it at home and yeshivah, it is obvious who the client is. The kid, right?

Then if the kid is the client, I need to ask him why *he* wants therapy (he doesn't; everything is fine as far as he is concerned…), and we will undoubtedly be very surprised at his answers. His answers will look very different than those of his parents. He will say, "I want my parents to stop bothering me about my hair or sneakers. I want to change yeshivos. I want a smart phone."

If the *kid* is the one coming to therapy, and the therapist is working on the *parents'* goals, the therapy is doomed from the start.

Now if the therapist is any good, she will understand that this client's presenting problem is wanting the new hairstyle or sneakers, but the underlying issue may be very different. Unhappiness. Self-esteem issues. Poor impulse control. Lack of communication with parents.

The therapist must contract with child and parents to achieve these goals. If the parents understand, great, but if not, three months later, when the boy is still wearing his hair long, the parents complain that therapy is not helping. Their goals and expectations are not aligned. There's a breakdown of communication. Because what is happening is that the boy for the first time is able to communicate his needs to an adult (the therapist) and for the first time is beginning to think of his future, and examine his present behaviors. But these are inner changes that are not yet manifested outwardly. There has been no more deterioration, but no external improvement either.

Or what if the teen has been self-harming and the parents are unaware? And the therapist, in order to maintain a therapeutic alliance, despite her best efforts to get her client to reveal his behaviors to his parents is still unsuccessful (usually because of terrible damage to the parent-child relationship)? The parents are still stuck on his sneakers, but the therapist knows her client has been successfully learning DBT skills that have reduced the self harming behaviors.

This idea of *who is the client* and *what are the goals* plays itself out when a husband is complaining about his wife's behavior and wants to see change, but when the wife comes into the therapy, there are underlying issues — of which her husband is unaware — that need to be addressed first.

Then there are unrealistic goals. A mother wants her daughter to conform to a standard of behavior that is presently beyond her capacity. To be ready for marriage. To achieve academically, socially, religiously. Perhaps the client has a learning issue, a social deficit, or is aware of the parent's religious hypocrisy and cannot live the double standard the mother effortlessly manages. How does a therapist confront this hypocrisy without alienating the parent? Or spouse, for that matter?

So the client begins to face his limitations. The hypocrisy. The client begins to assert himself. He does not allow himself to be pushed into a yeshivah or life for which he is not ready; while at the same time he does explore how he can be productive in his life. But the direction he takes is not in harmony with his parents, or spouse, who are paying for his therapy.

And then the client's family member decides that therapy is not working.

Therapy *is* working. Too well.

Other times, when a client talks about therapy not working, it is the client who is not working.

There is a concept in therapy to *be where the client is*. Begin the work where the client is ready to go. And sometimes there is no place at all to begin. Everyone wants the client in therapy except the client himself.

There is another concept of the therapist not working harder than the client to effect change. The client comes to therapy to make everybody happy. To say, "See? I am in therapy, so now you can't complain." But the client does absolutely nothing in therapy. Will engage superficially with the therapist, will avoid, come late, forget, pretend, ignore.

A smart therapist will call out the client on his behavior. A smart therapist would terminate and say, "Come back when you are ready."

Because when a client is not ready, when the therapist is working harder than the client, it's time to call it a day.

So how do you know if therapy is helping or if you are just wasting your time? You will know if therapy is helping. You came to therapy for a reason. So just check out if the reason you came in for is getting better. That's all. Otherwise, you are wasting your time.

But remember, the most important way to figure it out is to know what the problem really is. Not the fake problem. Not the presenting problem. The real deal.

When you open your eyes to the real problem, you will know if therapy is helping. If you actually use therapy to change, you won't have to ask; you will know.

Therapy Is Not Helping Me, Part 2

So therapy is not helping you. And you are not interested in hearing how it is your fault. Because you absolutely think that it is the therapist's fault and you do not want me to contradict you about that!

Okay, okay! Stop yelling at me. Am *I* the therapist that is not helping you?

I will agree with you. That it is your therapist's fault. Maybe even *my* fault if I am your therapist.

Because in my last column, when I spoke about therapy being ineffective, I placed the responsibility on the client, not on the therapist; and I agree that sometimes we therapists gotta take the blame when therapy just doesn't seem to work.

There are many things that therapists do that make us lose or fail our clients.

I am going to share some of them so that you can understand more of your own therapeutic experience enabling you to find a therapist, and therapeutic experience, that will work for you.

Boundaries, boundaries, boundaries.

It is crucial that a therapist maintain appropriate boundaries. The minute you feel uncomfortable with a therapist because the therapist self-discloses inappropriately, breaches confidentiality to your spouse, mother, sister, or rebbetzin who referred you, or over-identifies with your problem, you are going to want to run away from therapy.

I remember the first time my sister's aunt's mother-in-law's youngest child's granddaughter (you get the picture) was referred to me, I panicked and called my supervisor about taking on the case. "I may see her at a wedding!" I told her.

And although she is not of my community or culture, she was totally on target when she responded, "Mindy, if you are going to refuse clients from your community, you are going to be done before you even start!"

She was right. So right that when I made a wedding a half a year ago, quite a few clients received an invitation to my son's wedding with — and without — my knowledge.

It is true that many clients come in to my office hesitantly, worried that I know them or their family, worried how to avoid me at weddings, worried that I will talk to their principals, parents, or sisters; and it is part of our work to learn to trust, and more importantly, for me to be trustworthy.

So we are not going to chat about people we know, I will not self-disclose randomly (although I do self-disclose deliberately as a therapeutic tool), I will not meet her mother at a Chinese Auction and gush how wonderful her daughter is (even if we both know that her mother knows she is in therapy and is even paying for it, even if part of therapy is collaborative work between client and mother in and out of session), because that is a breach of boundaries. I will not listen to my client's story and over-identify or commiserate with her because then I will lose my objectivity. I must always remember my role as therapist even as we enter one of the most intimate relationships that exist.

There are other reasons therapy fails.

The therapist fails to help the client identify the reason for coming to therapy and formulate a plan to address the problem.

Sometimes, I find that teen clients have a different agenda than their parents for coming to therapy. So I put that out on the table for them. "Your parents want you to stop being disrespectful at home," or "They want you to wake up on time to go to school." But then I ask them, "If you are stuck in therapy anyway, what would *you* want out of this?" And she may say, "I really like this girl and don't know how to become friends with her."

And then we talk about how we can work towards the client's goals,

PART III THE THERAPIST AND CLIENT

but keep the parent happy anyway. Especially when this is exactly the friendship the parents do *not* want to encourage!

If I do not address the teen's motivation for therapy, then eventually I will lose her. And the reverse is true. If I do not remember that the parents are the ones paying for therapy, then I must keep the parents engaged on some level, while squaring that out with my teen client first.

Some dumb things therapists do is forget to ask what went wrong in previous therapies. Because if a client says how she hated when her previous therapist needed to reschedule her appointment, then I will immediately address what she needs from me if something should happen and I would need to do the same.

A therapist needs to explain how therapy works, or at least find out from the client what she thinks therapy does or how it works.

Clients sometimes have this weird perception of therapy and what my job is. Pretty early on, I explain how therapy works and what type of therapist I am. I often say, "If I am boring you, then tell me to keep quiet," and my clients laugh. Because on the one hand, I feel it's important for a client to understand on some level the therapeutic process, but on the other, often a client is not interested in hearing me explain. They came to talk and don't want me using up their time.

I especially need to prepare my clients for the emotional upheaval that may follow. After meeting a client once or twice, I can already gauge what issues may come up. A client may terminate suddenly because they have a hard time communicating their frustration, and if they get upset at me, they will quit rather than let me know. Other clients may need to be prepared for feelings of terrible anger toward me. Or even terrible feelings of love. By preparing them for these emotions, when they come, a client can think or say, "Oh, this is what Mindy was talking about," and their anger — or love — doesn't seem so scary anymore.

There's lots of other stuff a therapist could mess up with. Believe me, I know because I have made plenty of mistakes. But if I would have to end off here, there is one more I would throw in as primary in importance.

Therapists need to *elicit* feedback from the client about therapy, and they should be able to convey their absolute acceptance and ability to *contain* any negative feedback.

It would mean a therapist asking questions like, "How is therapy working for you? What do you need from me that is not happening yet? Do you notice feelings of frustration at me? At therapy? Are you ever angry at me?" and the message must be that the therapist not only does not mind negative feedback, but welcomes the clients' uncensored and open thoughts and feelings.

And sometimes, a therapist needs to apologize.

The honeymoon phase of therapy is right in the beginning when hope suffuses the therapy room. When the actual work begins, it becomes the sweaty, bloody work of two people in an imperfect world, the microcosm of the therapy room.

And both of us, therapist and client, must do our best. And sometimes even more.

PART III THE THERAPIST AND CLIENT

If I'm Paying for Therapy, I Must See Results!

You are paying me, for goodness' sakes.

And now that it's clear that you are a customer and that just as when you hire a contractor, plumber, teacher, or housekeeper, you expect results, and if not, you voice your complaints, you would do the same with a therapist. Right? Right.

Yeah, sure, you are thinking. *No way am I telling my therapist my complaints about her. I can't. Just can't.*

Last year, I attended a LINKS Shabbaton as the therapist-in-residence. For those of you unfamiliar with LINKS, it is an organization that offers support and other services (like weekend Shabbatons) for girls who have lost a parent. To be perfectly honest, I was not their first choice, but my friend and colleague who usually goes was unable to make it last year, and I was her substitute.

It was a tremendous eye-opener to me to how therapy is viewed by clients.

All day long (and way into the nights), girls approached me with questions about therapy. The most remarkable questions that I fielded over and over again were from girls grappling with their own therapeutic experiences, unsure how their therapist was helping them or if their therapist was helping at all. Some even had complaints about their therapists.

Again and again I told the girls, "Talk to your therapist. Tell her your doubts about therapy. Ask her your questions as to how she conducts therapy, how therapy is supposed to help. Tell her why you are unhappy with therapy, with her."

Again and again the girls looked at me, shocked, and said, "I can't say that! I can't criticize her!"

To me, it seems clear.

You called the plumber and the heat is still not working? Tell him. The cleaning lady left crumbs on the kitchen counter and it's sticky to touch? Show her what needs to be done. Your daughter is failing at math this year, even though she managed to keep up every year prior? Let the tutor or P3 teacher know her methods don't work for your daughter.

Why is therapy any different?

If a client is paying for therapy, she must see results. If she doesn't, she must discuss it with her therapist. That's all. Nothing more, nothing less is expected of any service given and paid for.

After that Shabbos, I tried to examine this phenomenon of a client's fear to demand accountability, transparency, and open, honest communication about the therapeutic process itself in order to empower clients to take charge of their therapy, and for therapists to engage clients in this process, which I believe will decrease drop-out rates and increase client success.

As a therapist, I have been greatly influenced by the works of Dr. Irwin Yalom, who has written many books unmasking the mystique of therapy. Perhaps that is why I entered my own practice with such forwardness. Within the first session or two, I usually ask my clients, "Do you have any questions about therapy? About my credentials? How I work as a therapist?"

I ask, "Once you start therapy, how will you know I am doing my job, that therapy is working?"

Along the road of the therapeutic relationship, I will often ask, "What criticism do you have about therapy? What is not working for you? What do you think I should be doing differently to help you? What is not helpful to you in therapy?"

I am not afraid of the answers because the client's ability to speak to me will foster a greater commitment to therapy and deeper therapeutic relationship that will enable her to achieve the goals for which she entered therapy to begin with.

I will say, "It seems like you are wondering why you came to therapy. Maybe you think you came to the wrong therapist. Possibly you are in middle of deciding to change therapists to one who can do a better job." And when the client looks surprised that I am reading her mind, I will say, "Do you want to talk about it?"

The client will ask me why she should bother talking about the things bothering her about me or therapy in general if she can just change therapists and avoid the hassle.

I explain.

"Maybe I truly am not the right fit for you," I will say. "Maybe another therapist will do a better job, or your personalities will mesh better, or her therapeutic orientation or style is more attuned to your needs. Maybe. So examining these aspects of what is wrong here will help you find the therapist you need without wasting more energy by starting again and again and again."

Sometimes, that will make sense to them.

Sometimes, they need to hear more. Because most of the time, they do not want to change therapists, they just want *me* to change, to be better, to help them more. Because they are feeling anxious and upset and don't like feeling this way and want me to help them change, fast. And faster.

So I will ask them what bothers them about me.

One client will say, "You talk too much. Be quiet so I can think."

One will say, "You allow too many silences in the room, and they make me uncomfortable. I need you to fill the silences with words."

When I hear these criticisms, I think about what they are saying. If there is merit to what they say and I realize I am remiss in some way, I address it directly. If I know that the issue lies with the clients, if, say, they need to learn how to hear what they have come to hear, or if I think the inability to sit with silence and with introspection is indicative of a deeper problem, then this gives me the opportunity to open dialogue with them.

I celebrate my clients' ability to critique me, to criticize me and to ask me what I am doing to earn the hard-earned money they give me. And I continuously seek to explain the process of therapy. Sometimes, I will say, "If you have such-and-such anxiety, you can save yourself a lot of money by just buying such-and-such book. You don't need to see me for that." Or I will say, "I don't think you need to see me so often. You are doing fine. What if we begin talking about termination?"

I like to help them speak about things they find difficult to say.

Even, "I think I have helped you as much as I am able to. Do you think you want to move on to another therapist?"

Their relief is palpable.

They worry they may hurt my feelings; they worry that I may get insulted.

Clients do not realize that therapists are more committed to doing their job than nursing hurts and wounds in the office. We do not get insulted when a client tells us that we are lousy at what we do. We use that information to help the clients understand how they are disappointed in us, in their parents, in their spouses, and how to improve expectations and relationships by taking responsibility for their actions, for their health.

We do not get affronted when our clients choose to leave us to see a different therapist; we want to help them find the right one who will be the right catalyst to improve their life.

As intimate as the therapeutic relationship appears, a good therapist thinks first and foremost of the client. And part of that is not only allowing freedom of speech in the therapy office, but inviting it, embracing it, being curious about it Through that dialogue, the client is empowered — and sometimes, sometimes, the therapist learns something new, too.

PART III THE THERAPIST AND CLIENT

Therapist Love

My client sits in front of me. We have been together two months or two years. She has cried in my office and laughed. Shared the most private moments, both ugly and beautiful. I have been privy to her deepest secrets, fears, joys, and loves.

Inevitably, what she wants to know is, "Mindy, do you care about me?" and underneath that questions lurks the real one she is afraid to voice. "Mindy, if I would not pay you, would you still care about me? If I would not pay you, would you want to see me anyway?"

In that moment, when I become aware of her question, whether she voices it aloud, or whether she whispers it in many ways, I seek to find a way to convey to her my answer, knowing she will not hear me anyway. She asks this question when she comes into session and she holds her back to me, methodically taking off her coat and placing it down so that she can take some breaths before entering into the therapy session. Gathering her thoughts and anxiety to turn around to face me. Or, as she sits, her fingers twist the tissue into tiny bits, her silence asking a million questions that I must mind-read. It is in how she hands her check to me with a smile or how she lays it upon the couch as if it is contaminated so that I must reach for it myself. It is when she cancels her session suddenly with no explanation and waits for me to ask the next week. It is how she accuses me of not caring when I do not pry for information, respecting her privacy and giving her space to tell me in her own time. She accuses me of indifference when I have just told her how I have researched schooling options for her and obtained the necessary numbers she can call.

Therapy, Shmerapy

In all these ways, both big and small, verbal and non-verbal, she shouts her question, "Do you care about me, Mindy? Do you? Do you really?" and if I say, in ways both verbally and non-verbally, "Yes, of course," she demands of me, "How do I know? Why should I believe you? You are only doing this because it's your job."

So this column is to share with you my thoughts, the words each of us therapists try to find to reach your hearts to let *you* know what we have always known. We care. We do. And they are not simply words but more like blocks of burning letters that we place upon our hearts branding ourselves with your essence.

But the question becomes sticky when you pair it with payment. If I would be your mentor, a volunteer, it would be so easy to believe me. If I receive no compensation, why I else would I spend time with you if not for loving you? In your mind, my fee corrupts the relationship.

So let's talk about that.

Remember those teachers you loved as a child. Did you ever feel that their warmth and giving was tainted by their salaries? What makes a therapist different?

Have you ever suspected you had cancer? Your child had cancer? And when you sat with the oncologist, you felt his concern and compassion? Was your appointment free and that is why you felt you could trust his words? What makes your therapist suspect when she does the same?

How do you know when you love someone? How do you know when someone loves you in return? Where do you feel it in your body? When your father ages and you are paying for his cleaning help, buying him groceries, bringing him food, do you doubt his love for you because you are giving him money? Can you only evaluate your relationship with your mother if your contributions are absent? Why is money tainting your perception of the therapeutic relationship?

I say this often and I will say this again: Therapists become therapists from an innate desire to help others, our natural ability to connect and bond. For most of us, we have been doing this work as soon as we entered grade school, always that listening ear for others, sensitive to the pain of others. Many of us consider ourselves lucky that we are getting paid to do the work we love. The money is a secondary gain, but not the primary reason we entered this field.

When I first began the journey into this field, I was aware that I would be working in an agency for $22 a session, if the client showed up at all, not including the hours of supervision and paperwork that I would be required to do. It never dawned on me that one day I would be in private practice and my chosen career would actually pay the bills. My dreams were about how I would help people, not about how I would make money doing it. And I think many therapists have similar experiences.

And when I sit with my clients who ask this question, I want to say, "How do you *not* see my caring?" In how I am here with you in your pain, how I respond as soon as I can to your emails or texts out of session, how I attend trainings and read books and pay for constant supervision to make sure I am giving you my utmost, how I often spend hours you are unaware of finding out ways in which I can help you, with your job, with your school, with your interests.

I ask you again, "How do you know when someone likes you? Cares for you?" and when you think about it, allow yourself to experience my caring as well. It is there plainly for you to see, to feel.

Once I read an article in which a therapist coined the word therapist-love. There is a love a child has for a parent, and a parent for a child. Teacher to student and husband to wife. And there is also therapist-love. I agree. There most definitely is. And you know it.

Part IV
The Family

Self-esteem is often that elusive need that derails us from reaching the tip of the pyramid. It is the need to be respected by others and to respect ourselves. We crave the respect of our parents, spouse, children, family, friends, and colleagues. Psychologist Abraham Maslow identifies a lower and higher level of self-esteem, in which the lower level is conditional upon the view of others and our interactions with those others, while the higher level is when our self-esteem is self generated and not dependent on others.

Many of my clients are burn victims, their skin so thin it takes months of respectful interaction to enable them to begin this process of acquiring self respect.

My own self-esteem as a fledgling therapist fluctuated constantly as I spent hours in session doubting myself, wondering if I would ever be good enough or smart enough to actually help anyone. And I am grateful for my supervisors who believed in me and taught me to believe similarly in my clients.

One supervisor also demonstrated absolute positive regard for me, and I have memorized her words that stand me in good stead as I meet with diverse clients from diverse backgrounds.

"To me," she always said, "being human, the humanness of people, transcends any other aspect of who we are, culturally, racially, religiously."

Therapy, Shmerapy

A Therapist Speaks to the Parents of Her Client

Dear Mother. Dear Father.

As your daughter's therapist, there is something I need to tell you. Because when you come to my office with your teenager, you are in pain. Your child is in pain. And something must be done.

I believe that the parents of my clients love their child passionately. I pass no judgment as to why your child needs therapy. (I have made my own mistakes with my teenagers, and we've all survived them.) The more important question is: How I can fulfill my responsibility to you once you've entrusted your child into my care so I can help her?

There is nobody in your daughter's life as important as you are. Nobody. I know that. You should know that, too. But teens are simply a species unto themselves. And until they turn that corner into adulthood, the sane rules of adult life just don't seem to matter to them.

So I need to explain what happens in the therapy room. What teens need in a therapist. And why a therapist working with teenagers is often in an untenable situation, navigating between the client, the parents, and sometimes also the school and various other individuals who may be involved.

Ideally, work with a teenager, as with any child, should be a collaboration between therapist, parents, and the teen client.

Ha.

I will tell you what I say to parents of new teen clients and what happens after that.

Initially, under the best circumstances, both parents will come in with their teenager. I am already enlightened upon seeing both parents. How they interact with each other, how they each interact with their daughter. How and where they sit, how and when they pay me. It's even better when I meet the parents before the teenager even comes in. In the second session, the parents come with their teenager and most things are repeated in front of the teenager. I then ask the parents to leave, giving me the second part of the session to hear from the teenager.

Once I get to talk to everyone, I will talk about confidentiality.

Here's my spiel: "Because your daughter is under 18, legally, you are allowed to know anything you wish to about her treatment." Then I turn to the teenager, "And legally, I can talk to your parents about anything you say or do in here." I complete my little speech, talking directly to the parents again. "Obviously, no normal teenager is going to talk to a therapist if they know that anything they say I can repeat to their parents. I mean, dumb a teenager is definitely not!"

So I go on to explain my system. Once this session is over, I encourage the teenager to take charge of her therapy. We will arrange together the session time and she will bring payment with her each session. If a parent feels that they need to speak to me, I will try to first contact the teenager to get a heads-up, and if not, I will not engage in the conversation until the teenager meets with me and identifies exactly what I can and cannot say, with me taking notes to ensure I get that right. I will also let the teen know the approximate content of any conversation with her parents. I explain that I must establish this kind of safety and confidentiality for the teen because the foundation of a therapeutic alliance is trust, and without trust, little work will get done.

Parents worry when they hear this. And they have very important questions.

"What if I need to tell you something very important and it would not be in my daughter's best interests for her to know I told it to you?"

My answer? Most of the time that is not accurate. If it's that important,

Therapy, Shmerapy

the teen must hear it. If the teen can't hear it, then even if it's important, once I am dishonest in the relationship, the therapeutic alliance is compromised and that will undo any potential positive outcomes such revelations would effect.

"How can the therapeutic alliance be compromised if my daughter doesn't know about the conversation?" the parent wants to know.

I say, "If a child cheats on a test, and the teacher never finds out, is there no rupture to the relationship between teacher and child? Dishonesty creates ruptures even when people don't know."

Then comes the big question. "How we will know therapy is helping our daughter if we cannot talk to you regularly?"

A parent knows therapy is working, not by what the therapist says, but by how the teen's behavior improves! "You will see it," I say. "That's how you will know."

Because if a parent is sending her teenager to therapy because of disturbing behaviors at home, at school, then the purpose of therapy is to change those behaviors. No one needs to *talk* about it to find out if it's happening — you can simply open your eyes and look.

Parents come in and tell me, in front of their daughter, what a close relationship they have with their daughter. They cannot imagine talking to me will bother their daughter.

And here's the part that gets sticky. Often the parents are right. Their daughter adores them. But the first thing the teens tell me when their parents leave the room is, "Don't tell them anything I say."

It's a teenage thing. Loving parents and yet needing their distance, their privacy, their right to therapy without parents invading their space.

I try. I really do. I try to tell the parents all of this. To say, "Allow your child the space she needs in therapy. I don't want to isolate you. There is no one who loves this kid as much as you do. And I want to work with you. I *will* work with you. But just give this therapeutic alliance a little time to sort itself out.

"Because when your teen feels safe in therapy, when she feels she can truly trust me, then she will trust me enough that we can work collaboratively without that trust being compromised. At that point she will be okay with me talking to you whenever, and she won't even bother giving me notes on what I can or cannot say. She will breezily leave it to my discretion. And she won't even check up on me anymore quizzing me on what her parents told me. She won't even want to waste her therapy time with discussion of that. She trusts me by then. She trusts her parents. She is on her way to health."

I once heard something beautiful: "Parents are not necessarily part of the problem, but they are part of the solution."

I believe that sincerely.

So help me help your teen by ensuring her privacy. If you can do that, you may soon become her confidante.

Thank you.

Therapy, Shmerapy

A Therapist Speaks to the Parents of her Client, Part 2

Hello, Father. Hello, Mother.

Glad you are back. As a therapist for teens, I can tell you it's always important when parents collaborate in a teen client's treatment. But it's a confusing situation. For the teenager who is unhappy and for the parents who often have no idea what is going on, what went wrong, or how to help their child.

There are no magic answers. But the role of the therapist is to be that knowledgeable person in assessing the mental health of a teen and implementing strategies to help that teen regain functioning in all areas of his life; and if he has never had functioning, to help him acquire it.

And if I wanted to talk to parents about confidentiality in a previous column, in this one I want to address another relevant topic related to teens in therapy. And the purpose — as always — is to help parents understand so that they can be a key support in the teen's life, instead of a crutch or an unwitting saboteur.

Parents sometimes misunderstand the role of a therapist.

Parents will sometimes think that the therapist is a teacher, that the therapist's job is to teach the kid how to behave. As if that was the problem — the kid simply didn't know how to behave, and if the therapist will explain the rules of behavior to the teen, everything will be just fine.

Yeah, right.

Parents sometimes think the therapist is some sort of Rebbetzin or Rabbinical Advisor. Like the only reason the teenager has been acting out religiously is because nobody explained to the teenager that he grew up in a religious home, in a religious community. And once the therapist explains that, it will be so clear to the teenager that he will become perfect in his religious observance.

Yeah, right.

Yes, I am a religious therapist. Yes, I obviously have values consistent with the religious community. Those values definitely include my belief that *Yiddishkeit* is beautiful and meaningful, that Torah life is a gift to a Jew, and that *halachah* is sacrosanct. And for any teenager who walks through my door, my values are in his face with my wig, with my modest dress, and often in how they emerge unconsciously in our sessions.

However, my role as a therapist is not to encourage a child to keep to the religious path. That is a role I leave to the parents, the school, and the various *mashpi'im* and mentors, Rabbanim and Rebetzins in a child's life. And this is why: When a teenager enters therapy, his religious acting-out has little to do with his religion, but with his unhappiness. As a therapist, I need to address the unhappiness, or any other motivations that are driving his acting-out. Once those issues are alleviated, the acting-out becomes a moot point. In the meantime, of course, the other influences in a child's life, the other positive role models can impress religiosity on him in different effective ways that work collaboratively with the therapy focusing on a teenager's mental health.

Most teenagers feel most comfortable within the religious life they grew up in, and if a child's religious development is not thwarted by negative factors such as lack of marital harmony, social cruelty of peers, abuse or trauma, or contact with familial/community religious hypocrisy, then the natural inclination of a person is to grow steadily within the religious parameters of their community.

Although, and I don't want to scare you, I am finding religious acting-out with teens where none of these are true and the teen is simply drawn to the magnetic pull of technology and is sucked into the abyss of all that is unholy without any specific intent.

But even when that happens, when the lure of the outside world beckons regardless of any negativity in the child's life, that breach of community/religious boundaries also originates from some unhappiness, despite no evidence of marital disharmony, trauma, or the like — unless the trauma is in the child's perception of life, which is often possible (as in a social injustice that wounds one child, which would leave another child perfectly intact).

So, parent, don't expect me to lecture to your child about the importance of keeping Shabbos or not buying a smartphone or not rolling up her skirt or sleeves when she leaves her home. Because what I will be doing is examining and exploring with your child what unhappiness drives her to think that happiness can be achieved with the desecration of Shabbos, or with an immodest skirt, or with an iPhone when there are thousands of content teenagers without those things.

Therapy addresses the future and what actions in the present may impact a future the teenager didn't even realize she wants. Or if a teenager cannot even envision a future, therapy gives her the tools and confidence to believe she has one.

Therapy even allows the teenager, in a safe environment, to express terrible thoughts she knows would horrify her parents or teachers, or even friends. Often, saying them out loud, giving them voice, is like a pin to let all the air out of those thoughts, allowing them to deflate, to float away, to become insubstantial in ways that when they were locked up in her heart and head they could not.

In the same way, parents sometimes think the role of the therapist is to knock some sense into her so she should think the way her parents think. Religiously, or otherwise. To explain to her why she should not fight with her older or younger sister or brother (as if she doesn't know!), or why she needs to help at home. Why she should stop moping in her room and why it's important to make a bigger effort to make friends in her new class or get involved in her school production.

Parents think the therapist should become the rule-setter. The explainer. The teacher.

But the therapist will fail to reach a teenager, much in the same way the parents, teachers, and older sisters have failed to make her act normal and stop fighting — if she uses the same techniques that have already failed!

A therapist is a therapist. No more, no less. And she uses her skills as a therapist to help the teenager uncover the roots of her unhappiness, to discover her resources, talents, and strengths; to give her tools to help her find her way back to emotional health.

Once that happens, all the other stuff, the symptoms of acting out behaviorally and religiously, no longer have a purpose and will be extinguished.

So, I'm no teacher, but did I teach you anything here?

Therapy, Shmerapy

Glue, Tape, and Documents: Not the Only Attachments

I love kids.

Mine.

The baby in the carriage on the checkout line in the grocery.

My nieces and nephews. My nieces' and nephews' kids.

The whole lot of them.

Which is why my clients' babies often find themselves in session when their mother can't find babysitters, when the hassle of a babysitter just makes getting to therapy that much harder, and when my clients just want to show off their delicious blue or pink bundles.

As a therapist, watching my clients and their babies, toddlers, or even school-age children gives me insight into their attachment styles. Into their ability to mother others even as they struggle with mothering themselves. And sometimes, where they are limited in their ability to be mothers. Insight into what had been lacking in their childhoods when they were mothered.

There have been a lot of studies done on attachment. And throughout my columns I have definitely touched on them. But my article on the borderline mother created such a traffic jam in my inbox that I wondered if my readers wanted to understand their attachment styles, how it may have evolved, and how it impacts their lives today in their relationships with others most important to them.

There are four basic attachment styles.

Secure. Ambivalent. Avoidant. Disorganized.

PART IV THE FAMILY

Let's talk about the kind of parent that produces each of these types of attachment styles.

Which type of parent produces a securely attached child?

A parent who is aligned with the child, in tune with a child's emotions, and consistently responsive to her child. It's the parent who feeds her infant when he cries, recognizes when a pamper needs to be changed, and is there when a toddler needs to be soothed with a hug, a kiss, and a smile. A parent who takes joy in her child's presence, coos to him, talks to him, notices when the sun is in her eyes, and moves the carriage to face a different direction. The child of this parent is confident in his ability to have his needs met.

The parent who is inconsistent — sometimes attentive and sometimes intrusive or overbearing — causes the ambivalent or anxious attachment style. The parent who doesn't allow anyone to touch her infant for fear of germs, deadly diseases, or a number of any feared consequences, but otherwise will ignore that same child's cries when she needs to be held, soothed, or simply talked to. Perhaps the depressed parent, the one who stays in bed feeling overwhelmed, but a few hours later will engage in baking cupcakes. The parent who involves herself in her child's activities with friends to the point of intruding on his privacy, then abandons the child to a strange babysitter without saying goodbye. This child is clingy and anxious, never sure how and when his needs will be met.

A parent who is unavailable or rejecting causes an avoidant attachment. The mother who finds her children annoying, spends long hours at work, rarely smiles at her child, has no interest in games or hugs or hearing about the child's day. Has no patience to feed her baby, who ends up with a propped-up bottle more often than not. Whose pamper is changed roughly, with disgust, robotically. This child knows his needs will never be met. There are no expectations anymore.

Disorganized attachment occurs when a parent ignores or doesn't even notice a child's needs to begin with, or when a parent's behavior is traumatic or frightening. Loud yelling. Slapping across the face.

Inappropriate anger. Inappropriate punishment. This child is confused, severely disorganized, because he has absolutely no clue as to how to have his needs met.

When a child grows up, these attachment patterns manifest in adult characteristics.

Do you recognize yourself in any of the following?

If you are able to create meaningful relationships and set appropriate boundaries with others —workmates, friends, spouse, and children — you probably have a secure attachment style. You do not worry you will be abandoned by those you love or that they will stop loving you. It's okay with you to be dependent on others when you need them, and also to have others dependent on you. You like getting close with others and are confident that others like being close to you, too.

Are you anxious, insecure, controlling, blaming, or unpredictable? In contrast to those traits, are you also sometimes quite charming? You may be exhibiting the ambivalent attachment style. You want to get close to others, but you always worry about not being loved enough. You are so anxious about being close to others that sometimes you try to merge completely into that person that you love. And inevitably, your smothering causes exactly the reaction you fear — that person withdraws from you.

If you are distant, critical, rigid, or intolerant; if you avoid closeness or emotional connections, you have the avoidant attachment style. You don't like being too close to others. You need your space so much you may as well live on an island. You can't trust others, you get nervous from closeness, you avoid being dependent on others, and you don't allow anyone to depend upon you.

Chances are that if you breed chaos around you, or you are explosive, insensitive, even verbally or physically abusive, your attachment is disorganized. You are untrusting even when craving security and attachment. And while you are reading this, you don't even realize you are reading about yourself, although your daughter who is reading this recognizes you immediately. You are often the borderline mother.

It can be helpful to know your attachment style; awareness is the first step in making changes to the three styles that impair relationships with the people that matter to you most.

Here are three ways to change your attachment style.

Believe it or not, the first way is to marry someone who has a healthy attachment style! So if you did already, embrace it and begin to learn from your spouse. Open yourself to realize s/he does not have the same insecurities and patterns you have and you can stop being anxious about being loved, you can stop avoiding your spouse for fear your needs won't be met. Because your spouse is securely attached and is actually capable of meeting your needs if you just allow him, if you begin to trust, if you also recognize your own attachment style and where your expectations are distorted.

A second method is self-regulation. You can become aware of your behavior, the thoughts and feelings that drive them, and the bodily symptoms that clue you in to those behaviors, and in that way regulate those negative emotions and thoughts to improve your daily actions. Journaling can be helpful. Mindfulness can do the trick. Self-help books and exercises. Choose one. Or ten.

A third way is to enter therapy. The therapeutic relationship is a reparative one. In a safe environment in which a therapist *knows* you, *sees* you, when your dysfunctional patterns begin to emerge, the therapist brings your behavior into the awareness of the here-and-now experience, allowing you to initiate changes. So if you avoid closeness with your therapist (avoidant), or if you become needy and clingy (ambivalent); even if you become critical, nasty, or untrusting (disorganized), your therapist will help you work through these behaviors in ways that your behavior changes will be manifested outside of therapy as well.

I noticed a funny thing. When I write my articles, I feel a connection to my readers. We know each other through the words on this page. Don't you feel the same?

Hey, are we securely attached or what?

Therapy, Shmerapy

When Friends Fly, and Clients Cry

Sometimes, I cannot breathe with their pain.

When I was a teenager, I lived with the misery of worrying about friends.

If I had them. If I lost them. What to do at any given second to keep them.

So I am no stranger to the social drama that makes up high school. But I absolutely do not remember ever feeling the complete annihilation my clients are describing in their social lives. And I do not say this flippantly. My teenage clients are experiencing such exquisite agony that it is derailing their lives.

Is it possible that teenagers today are so sheltered, so spoiled, so mollycoddled that any discomfort sends them reeling? Were teens of a generation ago so much more resilient that they rolled with the punches more effectively? *Who* is to blame for this? *What* is to blame for this?

Is it because girls are socializing today more through phone and email, creating superficial relationships, and are prevented from working on substantive ones?

I don't know. I honestly don't know.

I don't know the *whys* of this phenomenon. I just know that teens are entering therapy at a rapid pace to cope with what we always thought of as normal teenage angst regarding the ongoing cycle of friendships, inevitable break-ups, and cliques.

So what is the purpose of this column, you want to know?

To make parents aware of how the break-up of a friendship can cause

PART IV THE FAMILY

irreparable harm to a teenager and the importance of early intervention.

To educate teachers, principals, and other involved school personnel of the ramifications for a teen who experiences her social interactions as traumatic, and how the school can effectively intervene.

To speak to the teenager who is reading this so that she may realize that her acting-out behaviors are coming from her distress and she should reach out for help.

And I'm not even talking about bullying. The psychological damage of relentless bullying is well-researched. But no. Bullying is not causing all this trauma. This is simply the stuff of teenage angst, the social dynamics of friendships in flux. It's how girls are mean to each other, and some pay a higher price than others.

What I have been finding in my practice with alarming frequency is that girls who have been doing well socially and even academically will literally fall apart when a friendship ends abruptly. When her best friend, from one day to the next, simply informs her that they are no longer friends.

By the time parents come with their teen for therapy, they can usually identify the downward spiral of depression, listlessness, unhappiness, and then acting out from that fateful day when the former best friend announced her withdrawal from the friendship.

These are children. Their actions are thoughtless and often cruel. But not unusual in social settings like neighborhoods, bungalow colonies, schools, and camps. For the most part, if we look into the histories of our own childhoods, there was often that friend we lost interest in and dumped. Unceremoniously. There was crying and recriminations and sometimes parental or teacher involvement, but eventually everyone moved on. After all, we are talking about children. They fall. They get up. Today, the friend *du jour* is Suri; tomorrow it is Chedva. Unpleasant but manageable.

But I am watching teenagers who disintegrate after such a fall-out. They do not recover and move on. The spark leaves their eyes, and they lose interest in school or camp activities. They refuse to attend school.

Therapy, Shmerapy

A trauma has occurred, and it impacts their every waking hour. The symptoms of their distress are as obvious as the ear infection when a two-year-old pulls his ears, moans in pain, runs a fever, and refuses to eat. What we don't understand is what these symptoms mean.

It is hard to imagine that a broken friendship can give rise to symptoms that we have always thought of as trauma. But it's happening.

So what can we do?

As a parent, when you notice changes in your teen's behavior, address the issue immediately. Even if the friendship won't ever be repaired, the distress can be alleviated with validation and empathy from a parent. If that is not enough, believe it or not, it may be necessary to start new in a different class, or even a different school or camp. If your child tells you she wants to change, then listen to her. It may be easier to start again than to live with the source of the trauma day in and day out.

If you are the principal or teacher, it is crucial that you listen to parents who describe their daughter's misery and the enormity of the child's suffering, whether or not it makes sense to you. School performances or collaborative projects can often mitigate these symptoms by enabling a child to shine and make new friends in her new role. If a parent asks you to give her child a part in a performance, don't jump to an indifferent response of, "Your daughter needs to learn she can't have everything she wants." Or, "Your daughter needs to learn how to handle disappointment. And you, as her parent, need to help her learn that lesson."

If you are a teenager reading this and you recognize your misery is a result of a friendship gone awry, talk to someone. Your parent. Your teacher. Your therapist. There are ways to alleviate the misery even when the friendship is over. You will not remain 16 forever. There are many beautiful friendships waiting for you. You may always miss what you have lost, but people change. Your friend did. And now you must. It will be hard, but you can do it.

I am glad I am not a teenager anymore.

But I am also glad I am a therapist who can help the teenager I once was.

Acts of Betrayal: She Might Not Know, But the Relationship Will!

Of course, I have been tempted!

Her journal, diary, or story for school is right there in plain sight, and I am overcome with curiosity to read what my daughter writes.

So I will ask her.

If she says, "Ma-a-a-a! It's private," then I will tell Curiosity to please find another parent to drive crazy, because the answer is no.

Believe me, I battle with this. I want to know my children's thoughts, their feelings, what happened to them during the day, what makes them angry, happy, sad, or triumphant. I want to know what makes them tick, what makes them tock, and what makes them whirr and sometimes explode into many jumbled pieces of tangled wire, hard iron bolts, and loose screws.

To know all that, I guess I need to develop a relationship with my children. And then I won't need to violate their privacy with my snoopiness.

As a therapist for teens, I am amazed at how many parents see nothing wrong with reading their teenagers' private writings to find out what their teens are up to.

Whew! Wait a minute before you attack me! I know, I know, I've opened a can of worms, and nobody likes worms! (Especially because we learned as kids that if you cut one in half, each will grow into a full-size worm... doubling the worms!)

By the time a parent has brought a teenager into therapy, a problem already exists. For the most part, if there is a good relationship between parent and child, there is no need for the therapist (although, yes, yes,

Therapy, Shmerapy

yes, other scenarios can necessitate therapy, even if there is a good relationship!). The parent can do the work of therapy. But if the relationship and trust between child and parent is shattered, the therapist may become that person who shows the teenager how a trusting relationship between adult and child can be developed and used to the benefit of the teenager.

So the parent, who adores her child to pieces (because really, nobody loves a child more than the parent — not a teacher, friend, or therapist — and nobody doubts that!), is frantic with worry, is frantic to know what is happening to her teenager, to that special kid who just two years ago was happy and normal. She can't sleep at night, she can't eat, and she can't believe that her teenager has turned into this unhappy, grumpy, secretive person who is totally removed from her loving parents. And nobody in her right mind, not even a therapist, thinks for a second it isn't so that it is the parent who loves her child most, and who is the most invested in her life.

But the means by which the parent tries frantically to establish a toehold into her daughter's life — one of which is to read her private thoughts, her diary, her journal — causes even more damage to the relationship.

"How?" you ask. "My daughter doesn't know. She will never know."

When we engage in acts of betrayal, in violation of a relationship, even when the other party does not know, the relationship knows.

If a child cheats on every test and nobody ever finds out, do you truly believe the child's character and relationship with her peers, teachers, and parents is not being molded by her deceit?

Of course it is. You know that.

When a parent violates her child's privacy, even if the child never finds out, the relationship undergoes change and is shaped as well by the secret knowledge the parent harbors.

So you want to know, "How will I know what my daughter is doing, where she is going, what secrets she is hiding if I do not read her diary? How will I protect her from herself if I do not know?"

As a therapist, I will tell you that your knowledge does not change her actions or her ability to choose better, or to change and be the good daughter, the good Jew, the good person she needs to be. You cannot protect her from herself when she is on the downward spiral. You can only use the one ace you have. You are her parent, and you can love her like nobody else can or does.

Put your energies into reading your daughter, not her journals. Learn who she is, talk to her even when she rebuffs you, build the relationship even as she pulls it down again and again. Go to therapy to learn how to do this if I am speaking a foreign language to you.

You say you have no problems with your other daughters. You have a wonderful relationship with them. I do not doubt you. But if I may ask, is your relationship close with your other daughters? Or are you merely living in close contact with them? Do they share their hopes, their dreams, their disappointments, their opinions with you? Do you laugh together? Have fun? Do you have serious conversations with them about matters important to you, to them?

As a parent of teens myself, it's not as though I am so naive as to think my children would do nothing wrong. It's more that I trusted them that if they made mistakes, they would be capable of fixing them. So if I would suspect my child may have engaged in something I would not approve of, it would not be in my best interests to prove they did it or to triumphantly catch them at it. It would be more important to me to show them I trust them generally to make good decisions, and, if necessary, to make restitution.

By the time your teenager is in therapy and you are reduced to reading her private correspondences to herself, to others, your need to know is to assuage your own hysteria, not to assuage hers.

The wonderful thing about relationships with parents is that it is never too late to build, to rebuild, or to create. Teenagers want nothing more than a relationship with their parents, no matter what their behavior, facial expressions, or body language screams.

You are the most important person to your teenager. Don't spend your energies violating her privacy; invest in a trusting relationship that she will eventually prove she is worthy of.

Therapy, Shmerapy

Shidduchim and Therapy Secrets

There are two categories of people with whom I really need to have a heart-to-heart talk. And it may be you I am talking to, so listen up.

Lots of people are in therapy today.

No, I am not getting into a discussion about why there are more people than ever in therapy. All I am going to say on the subject is that people are refusing to be miserable any more than is strictly necessary. So today if someone is suffering, they will seek help to alleviate the suffering. Often with great results.

Gone are the days when children were socially isolated, bullied, experienced nauseous feelings before every test, or had headaches every time the math teacher walked in — and nobody cared or noticed. Gone are the days when marriages just coasted along, or strained relationships between family members were accepted as that's-just-the-way-thing-are.

Today, if there is a possibility of positive change (and there always is!), people go for help. People take their children for help. Children even take their parents for help. Neighbors, teachers, spouses, siblings. All are reaching out for help. For themselves. For loved ones.

Once, as I sat at a table during a wedding, I remarked, "If you look around this table, everyone single person here appears happy and successful. And often they are. But somebody in their family is not. And if I tell you that every third person sitting there has somebody in their family going for therapy, I would be grossly mistaken. Every **second** person has somebody in their immediate family going for therapy, and *every single* person has somebody from their extended family going for therapy (whether you know it or not)!"

And I love when the people I speak to exclaim in surprise that they actually do not believe it, because they are often unaware that their very own sibling, parent, child, or spouse is seeing a therapist.

Enough with all this.

Who am I speaking to right now?

To the unmarried adult client in therapy, and their parents.

Often, an older teen enters therapy for a variety of reasons that are impacting her functioning. She can be a great kid. Wonderful parents. Beautiful family. Sometimes despite the love the parents have for their child, there is a lousy relationship. Sometimes the parents are part of the problem, sometimes not. Whatever the issue is, the parents actually sacrifice a lot to send their suffering adult child to therapy to help her. And guess what? Therapy helps.

The client is happier socially, capable of getting a job, talks about marriage.

And then, miracles of miracles, the client gets engaged.

To a great guy from a beautiful family, and everyone is thrilled.

And she is yanked out of therapy.

Because it's a stigma to be in therapy, and nobody wants to ruin this bride's chances to be happily married. Plus, keeping a secret about therapy is wrong. So the best option? Terminate therapy! She is engaged anyway, so who needs therapy? Or she is already capable of dating, so she's done. Wasn't that the goal of therapy anyway — to make her marriage material?

No. No. No.

This is precisely the worst time to take a client out of therapy.

If a client terminates therapy, it needs to be done because she is finished and has achieved her goals. Not because she is entering *shidduchim*, or because she is engaged, and it is a secret she cannot tell her fiance, prospective fiance, or new husband.

Often, the issues a client comes into therapy with are ones that are either exacerbated with new stressors, or must be reworked with a new stressor. For example, if a high school student suffers from anxiety, from social issues, from anger management, from indecisiveness, therapy will be very effective at that time. But often, if the new stressors come up too soon after, such as parents divorcing, a new move, graduating, entering the work force, becoming engaged, married, or pregnant for the first time, the results have not been fully solidified and may come up again in a different form.

The good news is that the foundation of therapy allows for quicker and better results, but the new stressors definitely need to be addressed.

As Rabbi Dr. Abraham Twerski once said "Marriage is not a hospital."

Being engaged or newly married is not the solution to a person's issues. It is often a stressor that can actually exacerbate the issue itself!

Or if a person is in middle of therapy, the issues of marriage need to be addressed in ways that were not relevant beforehand when the client was in high school or before *shidduchim*.

Practically speaking, what is the family to do when therapy is stigmatized and continuing therapy can cause one of two problems? Its stigma can jeopardize a girl's *shidduch* prospects. And if continued secretly, during the engagement or after marriage, it can undermine the very foundation of that new relationship which should *not* have secrets.

This is a tough question.

But not tough enough that there are no solutions.

In my experience, when working with such a situation, continuing therapy and revealing the secret does not impact *shidduchim*. But it needs to be addressed case by case on an individual basis. Many factors play a role in how to achieve this. It is important to assess the culture to which this client belongs. If she is engaged after one *b'show* or three and then does not meet her *chassan* until the wedding as in Chassidish circles, or if she is meeting or talking weekly as in the Litvish circles; or any other variation thereof.

It goes without saying that the guidance of a Rav before *shidduchim*, during *shidduchim*, and once a girl (or boy) is engaged is crucial. But just as crucial is the collaboration between parents/client, Rav, and therapist who can each contribute to understand the nature of the situation and best address it in the context of the continued need for therapy, the problem of stigma, the detriment of secrecy, and the desire for a successful marriage. When to say. What to say. How to say.

I speak to the parents of these clients. To the clients themselves. I speak to the potential in-laws of these clients. I tell them that they have still gotten the best *shidduch*.

And I will tell them that if they cannot work this out, often, neither will the marriages.

Therapy, Shmerapy

A Note to Our Sponsors (of Spirituality)

Just for the record, let me say that I am awed by our community. I should say communities, plural, but that would imply divisiveness, and I am loath to put to paper any indication of that. Although we have our issues, I applaud our wonderful schools, principals, and teachers who are dedicated, invested, and involved in their students' lives.

I met a *menahel* of a yeshivah who told me how he keeps an eye out for students who come in during those pre-Pesach days without having eaten breakfast at home to start off their day.

"Their mothers are simply overwhelmed," he told me. "It's the married children moving back from Eretz Yisrael, it's the preparations for Pesach, the cooking and cleaning. And these little kids come off the bus hungry."

"Guilty." I laughed. "I was one of those mothers last year!"

He didn't think it was funny. "I make sure those children go down to the lunchroom and get food," he said.

I have spoken to principals who not only arrange for therapy for students in distress, but pay for it as well. Other teachers arrange for private, free tutoring, and I have met the most unbelievable teacher who washes her student's uniform so that the child has a freshly ironed and clean uniform shirt, free of stains indicating what she ate the day before.

How can I not love our schools and teachers?

It is because these people love their students so much, care so much, that I would like to address an issue cropping up frequently in high schools that I am hearing about from my teen clients. I have no doubt that any teacher who recognizes herself in this column will understand the problem and figure out a way to address it.

So here it is.

I would venture to say that there are quite a number of students in therapy. A handful in every class or grade, surely. Often very talented, popular, wonderful girls who no one would dream would ever go to therapy. Or would ever need therapy. But these brave girls battle anxiety, depression, difficult home situations, or life challenges. They reach out for help because they are successful and expect nothing less for themselves. They are often top students, well-groomed, pretty, social, and gifted. They sing, dance, play music, act, create, and write.

Of course, there are other students in therapy too, such as those who appear unhappy, are not doing well socially, are experiencing ambivalence about Judaism, and come from unstable homes. But I am addressing the teachers of the seemingly well-adjusted, successful students who are in therapy — or who are seriously contemplating therapy for various reasons.

And here's the problem:

In the fiery enthusiasm of their lessons, teachers unwittingly make hurtful and disturbing comments that send their students in therapy reeling.

"Girls!" they say. "All therapy is in the Torah! You don't need to go to therapy to understand how to live a good life! The Torah tells you exactly what to do! Keep the *mitzvos,* and you won't have any anxiety or depression!"

Or, "*Yelados yekaros*! If you just have enough *emunah*, then everything will be good! Learn to trust Hashem, and watch your life be wonderful!"

Or, "*Kibud av v'eim* can be a difficult *mitzvah* sometimes, but you need to work very hard to do it! No excuses! There's never a time to say *no* to a parent! *Chas v'shalom*! If a parent tells you to do something, even if it is hard for you, then you must do it!"

How about this one? "The Torah tells us how long to grieve for a loved one. First comes the funeral, then seven days of *shivah*, then thirty days

Therapy, Shmerapy

of the *shloshim* and then for a parent, a year of *aveilus*. After that, enough! It is time to move on!"

Now, just for the record, I will say that I too was a wonderful teacher in a different lifetime. And I was guilty of a lot of dumb mistakes. I still feel guilty about an early year as a teacher when one of my students had mono (mononucleosis). And when she returned to school, because she looked fine to me and because I really had no idea what mono was, I acted inappropriately when my student did nothing for the rest of the year. Stuff like rolling my eyes and not believing her when she explained that she was too tired to do anything except come to school and sit there. I was clueless to the fact that simply showing up each day took great effort and that she would have loved to be able to do homework and take tests and write notes, but she simply could not.

And that is why I will never judge teachers who have made these comments. They simply do not understand. And that is what this column is for — to give them tools to understand their students so these comments should not cause the damage they do.

So what is the problem with those seemingly innocent comments?

Here's this special kid sitting in class who is undergoing tremendous challenges, and her parents, her parents' Rav, and her own principal have recommended that she go to therapy because the problem is too big to handle herself. She is a *frum, ehrlich* girl who wants to do the right thing. And then she hears her teacher saying that if she would just try harder to have *emunah*, then she would not be feeling these panic attacks. Imagine how that destroys her fragile sense of self. Therapy becomes proof of her failure to have sufficient *emunah*, instead of a tool to help her *avodas Hashem*.

The same is true for the other comments. The child in therapy who is dealing with an incredibly difficult home situation in which she is unable to practice *kibud av v'em* in a normal way, who is grieving, or who is suffering from anxiety or depression, is broken by such words that fault her. Even when she is receiving support from others who validate her struggles and reassure her that her *emunah* is strong, her grief is normal, and her *kibud av v'em* is an admirable work in progress.

Today, when so many students are in therapy, when so many of their family members may be in therapy, it is possible we have encountered a new dimension of how we must teach these monumental concepts, such as *emunah,* by acknowledging the role of therapy in the lives of many children and phrasing our words differently in the classroom.

Thank you, principals and teachers, for listening. We are all messengers here to help make the world a better place for the innocent souls in our care. We must work collaboratively to help these children that we both love and care for very much.

Therapy, Shmerapy

A Coupla Stuff About Couples

Couple counseling is fascinating work.

If sitting in a room with *one* client is dynamic, imagine what it is like with *two*. The interesting part about couple work is that the couple, not the individuals, is the client. Sounds weird? It is a novel concept, but one that every therapist needs to bear in mind.

Say I am seeing a woman for therapy and after a time, she decides she wants to bring in her husband for therapy. To work on her marriage. Sounds simple. "Why not?" you say. "Why start from scratch by going to another therapist when you already know everything and can begin the work so much quicker?"

You make sense, but such a scenario is a pretty sticky one, and I will tell you why.

If my original client is the wife, then the purpose of bringing in her husband for couple counseling must be identified.

Is it a one- or two-time occurrence to work on a specific situation? If yes, I would not consider that couple counseling, but rather a collateral session in which the wife still remains my primary client and her husband is only there to help improve her life in the ways he can. He is simply a collateral to his wife's therapy.

But what if the purpose of bringing in the husband is to stop individual counseling to work on couple issues?

If that's the case, then the entire dynamics of the therapy must change from individual work to couple work, and that means the wife is no longer my client, but the couple is. It may sound like simple semantics, but the way couple sessions would then evolve would be totally different from a therapeutic perspective.

Honestly? I don't like to make that shift. Even when the second spouse comes in only as a collateral to the individual work, there is much groundwork that needs to be laid to make sure that therapy remains a safe place for my client. If my client agrees to lose her individual therapy status and allow for the couple to become the client, I need to carefully prepare her for that shift, how it may affect her, and how to navigate such a change. I rarely do this, and only when I assess that it is in the best interests of a client who is asking me for this change. Otherwise, I do all I can to encourage transferring to another therapist for counseling, even if my client does not return to individual counseling as a result.

And if my original client wants to engage in couple counseling and then come in for individual counseling in addition to that, it becomes even more complicated. I don't say I would never do it, but it is a case-by-case evaluation how to ethically and responsibly balance these changes.

So how else is couple counseling different?

All therapists have their orientations as to how they view individuals and their problems that bring them to therapy. Similarly, when faced with a couple as a client, there are different orientations we can adopt in order to understand the couple and its problems.

Here are some examples:

An object relations/attachment model of couple counseling will focus on each spouse's attachment patterns to his and her parents. According to this theory of therapy, a person will not marry the person he wants to, but the person that he needs to. We marry the person who will replicate or heal or control or cancel out or live as the parent we wished we had as a child. We unconsciously try to use our marital relationship to achieve that which was unfinished from our childhood.

It might look like this:

A wife is always nagging her husband to be on time. Her husband is a caring, responsible, helpful person who has a chronic lateness problem.

To rectify a past in which she never made it to any school parties or functions on time because of her father's obliviousness to her needs, the wife has subconsciously married a man who has the same chronic lateness issue that her father had.

Never mind that her husband is not her father, and he comes through in many other ways. Or that she is perfectly capable of driving her children to their functions, or she could easily afford to send them with a car service, or they have many good friends who would happily pick her up — in contrast to her mother who could not drive, or did not have the money to afford car fare, or whose friends lived too far to get rides from. No. This wife is getting stuck on a specific aspect of unresolved issues with her father that is playing itself out with her husband's lateness that really does not need to impact her with the severity she is displaying.

A trans-generational model of couple counseling is when a therapist views the couple's problems as part of a pattern embedded in the family over generations. If you do a genogram (an assessment tool that gathers information not only about a client but generations prior), for example, what will emerge is dysfunctional patterns of familial functioning. A pattern, for example, of divorce in each generation that will also show a cut-off between the non-custodial parent and the children. So a therapist would look for those same patterns in the present to see how the couple relates to each other.

Other models of couple's therapy are experiential approaches, such as Gestalt therapy, in which the therapist views the couple's issues in context of how each makes meaning of their existence in the here-and-now. As wife, as husband, and how those worldviews influence both their behaviors in the present and how they move into the future.

An example of this would be understanding how each member of a couple understands his/her role as a religious wife or husband, what is expected of him/her, and how closely aligned these expectations are with his/her spouse's, and most significantly with his/her own expectations. If a woman wants to stay home and take care of her children rather than work, but her husband wants to learn in *kollel*, then these expectations will cause friction in the relationship.

Here's one more.

A structural model of couple counseling focuses on the transactional patterns of how the family is structured and relates to each other. Every family creates its own internal pattern of organizing itself, has a set of rules by which it operates, and has subsystems of relationships which allows for overall family functioning, whether functional or dysfunctional.

A therapist viewing a couple's problems through a structural perspective is interested in understanding how the family works. Who brings home the money? Who takes care of the house? Who disciplines the children? The therapist wants to know the rules of the house. Like, creativity takes precedence over cleanliness. We wash our hands before dinner. Homework is important/not important. We visit Bubby every week, or we never visit Daddy's parents. The therapist wants to know the spoken and unspoken rules that have evolved over the years and created this family's structure and behavioral patterns. Also, the therapist is interested in the family subsystems. Who is a pair in the home? Mommy and Totty? Or is it Mommy and Moshe, the oldest son, and Totty is ignored. Is it Totty and Chavie, the middle daughter and Mommy is ignored? When Mommy says no more candy, do the children pair themselves up with Totty who says yes?

A couple brings drama into the room in a way that the individual, who only brings one perspective into therapy, cannot. It is the therapist who becomes the director of this drama. But the therapist, as well as the couple, would need to know first which script they want to use.

Therapy, Shmerapy

Family Fun Time: When Therapy Can Flummox the Family

Just when you thought you knew everything you needed to know about therapy for individuals, I am going to give the rug underneath you a little jerk and topple you over with another model of therapy called *family therapy*.

Yep, you heard right. Family therapy is when the *family* comes into the therapy room.

Yeah, I know.

Just imagining yourself in therapy was a major step. Now the idea of your parents, your husband, your kids, your sister-in-law or son-in-law in therapy is enough to send you to a psychiatrist for some medication or sleeping pill that will put you out of commission for a coupla years.

I happen to love doing family therapy. And I will tell you why.

Here's what happens:

Parents drag their kid into therapy and say, "Fix him!" Or schools mandate a child into therapy and command, "Get this girl functioning again."

Sometimes, the script changes, and a man sends his wife to therapy, or a wife sends her husband. Or everyone points a finger at the father, accusing him of being the problem, or at the new daughter-in-law who has upset the family somehow or another.

These individuals are called the *identified patient*. It's easy to see why this or that individual has been identified as a culprit, wreaking havoc in the family. She is sulking in her room, barking at her siblings. He is waking up late for morning prayers, refusing to attend morning classes at yeshivah. She is yelling at the children. He is withholding money from his wife. And the new daughter-in-law refuses to join the family for Shabbosos, holding her husband hostage in her home.

Right?

Wrong.

Often, when these individuals come for therapy, a clearer picture emerges in which a family system of dysfunction is revealed. The child is socially awkward or shy, but there is a family history of social maladaptation in which the mother has suffered socially all her life, but the effects were muted by her life of privilege that compensated. The sister-in-law is behaving badly, but then stories of the father's inappropriate behavior at the Shabbos table are revealed. And sometimes, the family's dysfunction is much more subtle and harder to identify.

As a mentor years ago for Project YES, which helps families-at-risk, my supervisor called these identified patients the weak link in the family. He compared it to a chain made up of links. Put a weight onto the chain, he explained, and eventually, one link will snap. The weight is felt by everyone, but one link will bear the burden of the weight. That is our identified patient, the kid or mother or sister-in-law who finally snaps under the family's burden.

In our community, we deal mostly with the identified patient, often with success, because when one wheel begins to move, the interconnecting gears begin to move as well (the other family members). But it is extremely gratifying to work with the family as a whole.

And in family therapy, the therapist's client is not the identified patient, but the family itself.

Each family has its own structure, rules, and self-regulating mechanisms to maintain the family's status quo — its homeostasis.

Structure would define how the family organizes itself — who is the boss in the house (or boss-driver!), the breadwinner, the religious authority, the disciplinarian, etc. Rules would define who needs to do what and why.

Therapy, Shmerapy

For example, rules would include religious and educational expectations, who needs to help and how, and other ways in which a family operates.

A functional family's rules, even those that are covert or unspoken, benefit the members of the family, such as, "We all have jobs to help prepare for Shabbos," or "Daddy is responsible for the rent and bills." In a dysfunctional family, rules can be givens like, "It's safer to stay in your room when Mommy is angry," or, "Girls have to help but boys can get away without doing chores."

A family can be a functional family but then become disorganized because of a challenge such as a death, divorce, loss of job, or illness.

Often, when an identified patient is brought into therapy, it's because she challenges the homeostasis. She upsets the family balance and how it has organized itself to function. A child is acting out at school, stealing money, and bullying. She is upsetting the family's rules in which children are expected to behave and not bring attentions to themselves. This rule is important to the family because then the father can cow the children into submission with his anger and threats of withholding.

According to the family, the child needs therapy to stop her behavior and return the family to its status quo. But therapy can cause more problems because the child is not necessarily the problem, although she is the identified patient! Sometimes, therapy helps the child act functionally and refuse to accept rules that are detrimental to her well-being, such as "We don't tell anyone that Totty and Mommy fight and say hurtful words to each other." This can definitely cause chaos when the child does tell!

If a therapist is successful with the child, then the family might find itself totally disorganized because this child is now healthy and will not abide by the family's dysfunctional rules and structure. That's when the kid is usually yanked out of therapy.

But bring the whole family into the therapy room, and a therapist can work with the family unit to effect change to the family that will restore the family's functioning, or enable it to find — for the first time — functional ways of achieving its equilibrium.

PART IV THE FAMILY

Therapists view the family through different lenses, depending on their orientation, and sometimes work with a few lenses. There's understanding how a family functions according to *inter-generational patterns* (the grandmother had anxiety, the mother has anxiety, the kid has anxiety), or perhaps through the family's *transactional patterns* in which we observe the hierarchical subsystems of the family (are Daddy and Mommy a strong dyad, or has the family restructured so that the oldest daughter and Mommy are aligned, leaving Daddy powerless on the outside?).

Family therapists use a variety of techniques and interventions to restore a family's equilibrium. One of my favorites is observing how family members seat themselves, revealing how they align themselves in the family. One child sits alone, another sits sandwiched between both parents. Two sisters sit together, a third sits furthest away from the family. A father sits near his daughter, the mother near her son. Chairs are angled away or towards each other.

And then sometimes, a therapist can simply move members nearer or further from each other to foster sibling or parent dyads, new alignments, and support systems that change the family's structure and bring it closer to healthy functioning.

The challenge of family therapy is channeling the dynamite to make it dynamic!

Part V
The Therapy

Self-actualization is the highest level of the hierarchy. It means knowing our potential and seeking to fulfill that potential. Once we are able to have our lower-level needs met, we are free to develop our higher levels of functioning. We no longer have to fight for survival or safety, for love or respect. We turn our sights to becoming the most we can be with the talents and resources we are given and have acquired.

"I want to hear a mother talk about her baby," a client once said to me.

She knew me from the community, and she had heard that my first grandson had just been born. I understood her need, as she had never been told stories of her own babyhood, and her transferential feelings toward me as mother were very strong. So I modeled for her love and expectation for the future, using self-disclosure with which I felt comfortable.

I talked about my new grandson, how I felt his weight in my arms, how he appeared completely formed, so "there"; the potential inherent in him, his wispy strands of hair...

"I wish you could talk forever," she said. "The warmth of your voice spreads over me like a protective shield." She sighed. "The 'how' of loving is not easy to define."

Neither are all the components necessary for self-actualization.

As a therapist moving my clients toward termination that comes with successful treatment in therapy, I remember D.W. Winnicott's metaphor, comparing termination to skating: It's not a gradual process because the only way to skate is to take your hands off the wall. To ride a bike, someone needs to let go.

And the most beautiful portrayal of self actualization is the perspective of a client who shared these words that have found their way into many therapy sessions with subsequent clients.

"I thought that I can take away the pain in my heart.
But I realize that what I can do better is enlarge my heart
with appreciation for life,
to recognize my own gifts to myself and others,
to open myself up to relationships and the exchange of caring
that my heart becomes so large,
the pain occupies such a relatively small amount of space that
it becomes insignificant."

My client's words have become part of her self-actualization and have found their way into the hearts of the many others with whom I have shared them. And I thank her, as I thank all my clients, for their willingness to teach me so that I can grow continuously toward *my* fullest potential as a therapist and person.

PART V THE THERAPY

Going Public on Private Practice

I have a hard time charging for my services.

A client comes in to my office. Very soon it's obvious that the fee for each session is difficult to come by. And inside, it hurts me because I know that it may take a few weeks, even a few months, and sometimes a few years, to address the issues that bring the client into my room. I know that money is needed for Yom Tov clothing, for a night out with a spouse, for a birthday present for a child. And often, if I feel the client may be receptive, I gently say, "You know, if money is tight, you can go to an agency and obtain a therapist there. It won't cost you anything because they will take your insurance, your Medicaid or Family Health Plus. Or at the minimum, it will be affordable, if you don't have any insurance at all."

But for the most part, my clients refuse to even entertain the idea.

Sometimes, when approached by a Rav, a principal, or a concerned neighbor, I encourage them to try to convince the shul member, the student, the family, to find a therapist at an agency, so that the Bikur Cholim organizations, the neighbors, the school, should not have to be burdened with paying for therapy that can be obtained for free. And I don't think I have ever been successful.

But now, I have a forum and I will try once more to educate our community about therapy through clinics and agencies versus therapy in private practice. And even though I may get angry letters from colleagues, from the agencies themselves, or even from my own clients, I must speak out.

I can speak because I worked in an agency before I went into private practice. And I was a very good therapist there and helped many people. And they got my services for free.

Here is what I can tell you about an agency:

There are many rooms and many therapists, and there is a waiting room where you wait until your therapist calls you into the room. And if you come pretty much on time, then the wait is also pretty short. Although yes, your privacy is compromised because there are other people sitting there and they may see you.

And yes, it is true that therapists in an agency can be less experienced than those in private practice. And sometimes you may get an intern (a student therapist who is still in school, before graduation), and that intern may leave at the end of the school year if they need to move on to another internship or because she/he was offered another job someplace else. True.

But I can tell you that as an intern and then as a new therapist, what I lacked in experience, I made up for in voracious reading and accessing available supervisors. I made up for my inexperience with my idealism and desire to help. And when I was an intern, legally, I informed my clients of my status, and none of them turned me down. (Although it is within your right to request not to be assigned an intern and your request must be honored.)

For the most part, the most important aspect of therapy is the relationship between client and therapist. Without the therapeutic alliance, no intervention can be successful (unless pure CBT is used). So yes, the intern or new therapist may know less, but armed with her ongoing education, access to frequent supervision, and awareness of her limitations, she can still deliver adequate, and even superior, therapy if she uses her most important tool: the therapist's self.

Really, there are quite a number of dedicated, seasoned therapists working in a clinic. Wonderful, professional therapists who sometimes also have a private practice apart from their work at the clinic.

A crucial benefit of receiving therapy in an agency is that due to the umbrella structure under which a client is treated, there can be collaborative work among therapists treating different family members, community and government resources can be accessed, and there is a system of checks and balances that protects the client.

A drawback is, as we said earlier, a drop less privacy, and also extensive paperwork that is required. After each session, there are notes a therapist must write, and there are treatment plans that must be written up. Both of these are done in private practice, but not necessarily in such detail (but that would depend on the individual therapist, as well). Treatment plans can be verbally agreed upon and notes legally need not be lengthy. But in any case, you can ask to see, or write those notes together with your therapist at an agency, to have some measure of control over what enters your chart.

As a therapist in private practice, I have noticed that paying a therapist each week sometimes facilitates improvement in functioning much more rapidly than when no payment is required. But I have also noticed how the drop-out rate is higher when there is no more money to continue paying for therapy, and a client is left hanging, with more damage done than good when therapeutic relationships are severed prematurely. People stay in therapy for a shorter duration, almost as soon as they obtain relief from their symptoms, whereas at an agency, they will continue longer to obtain the complete benefits of therapy because they are not pressured with payments.

I would be remiss not to address the obvious: therapists in private practice often have specific areas of expertise and skills that make their services invaluable. Yes. However, sometimes in an agency, there are specialized therapists, as well. You need to ask.

If money is not an issue, then yes, private practice is usually optimal. But if money is difficult, and you must pay a therapist weekly, especially when multiple family members need therapy, then the relief of not having to pay facilitates change in ways that the pressures of paying can undo.

I have seen both sides of the coin. There are no easy answers. But there are good questions you can ask to make your decision the right one.

Therapy, Shmerapy

Therapus Terminexus: Why Didn't You Say So?

Personally, I don't hold a gun to anyone's head, forcing them into my room for therapy. Maybe parents or spouses do that, but not me. So when new clients come into my office, even the ones who made their own decision to make that first appointment, they oftentimes walk in the door as if it was a holding cell until their execution.

Inevitably, they ask the question: "Okay, I'm here. But for how long?"

Am I supposed to feel successful as a therapist that somehow in the short time we have met, they have just realized their sentence has been commuted from death by therapy to a prison sentence?

And this is the myth that circulates about therapists: Since we get paid every time a client walks into our office, we wouldn't ever want that client to get better and terminate therapy.

So my clients are often very sure that entering therapy is a life sentence.

Unfortunately for me, as much as I try to make a living, my clients quickly get on with their lives, getting back on track, so that their therapeutic journey barely covers the price of the new tennis court I have long wanted to build on the roof of my home. Or the swimming pool I figured I may as well dig out in my basement. It's very frustrating for me, as you can well imagine. It would be so much more rewarding for me if my clients hung around at least long enough so I could finish paying off the mortgage on my house.

Therefore, when my clients finally ask the question as to how long therapy will take (and if they don't, I will usually bring it up), I actually do have an answer. "You will be in therapy for approximately sixty-seven years, give or take a few months for good behavior."

Just kidding!

My answer is pretty standard.

"Within a session or two, you will begin to feel hope that life will actually get better. Within two or three sessions, your symptoms of distress will begin to decrease. Then we will begin the journey to improve your functioning while continuing to alleviate anxiety and depression. You will begin to solve the specific issues you bring to therapy, as well as learn tools to apply to a wider variety of situations."

I don't necessarily use the same words, but the gist is always the same.

I say, "After a short amount of time, maybe eight to twelve sessions, you will feel you have accomplished what you had wanted when you first came in. At that point, you will choose to terminate therapy or decide you want to achieve even more than you had dared hope you can achieve. And then you can continue with therapy for as long as it is useful to you."

For individuals who come in for trauma work, the same applies, except that since trauma has an impact on so many areas of a person's life, therapy for that takes longer. For deep-rooted trauma, two to five years is a normal length of time for a therapeutic experience (although positive change is occurring regularly), but when the traumatized client finally has the courage to ask how long therapy will take to cure her, she is usually relieved to hear my answer of five years. It validates her knowledge but paradoxical disbelief that terrible things have been done to her.

How does a person know when to terminate therapy? When does a therapist?

The beauty of a therapist working first in a clinic setting before entering private practice is that the therapist gets to know who she is as a clinician when money is not a factor — as the clinician gets paid by the agency and not the client.

This is what I learned about myself: I will not force a client to terminate. However, if I feel I am no longer being helpful in some significant way, I may recommend a transfer to a different therapist. It could be because the client entered therapy at one stage of her life, made wonderful strides, but now needs another therapist, who will meet her at her new level of functioning, to move her onto the next level.

I may refer someone to another therapist when a client wants to try a different type of therapy in which I am not trained or if the therapeutic relationship is not a productive one. Therapy is like a *shidduch*; there needs to be a click between client and therapist. And sometimes I am simply not the right fit for a client. And that's okay. Ethically, it's the right thing to help a client transfer to a new therapist who may be the right *shaliach* to help in ways that I may not be able to. The client is not terminating therapy, but simply terminating with one particular therapist.

So if *I* don't terminate a client's therapy, then how does a client know when it is the right time?

Clients figure it out very nicely. It's when they have accomplished their goals in therapy that had been clearly delineated in the beginning sessions and assessed periodically.

As a therapist, it's easy for me to see the signs that a client is ready to terminate. It's when her life becomes so full and busy that she arrives to appointments late and then calls to cancel altogether. It's when she radically changes from creating her whole week's schedule around therapy to trying to fit therapy somewhere in her life. These are good signs, and I make my client aware of how her behavior is signaling to her that it's time to terminate. (These same behaviors can also be signals that the client is avoiding therapy because she feels it is not helpful but doesn't know how to confront the therapist with her fears and doubts — more on this in another article!)

Termination may be painful, but the concept is built into the very beginning sessions of therapy.

By the time a client is ready to leave therapy, she is kind of hoping I will adopt her and she can serve out her life sentence in my office.

If she sponsors an ice-skating rink in my backyard, I may seriously consider it. Otherwise, we work out a plan for termination and learn to say goodbye, so that termination doesn't have to mean loss, but rather a positive internalization of the therapeutic experience that will continue to impact her years after termination.

It's a wonderful feeling walking out of the prison her life once was. Case closed.

Therapy, Shmerapy

Controversy About Consent: When Parents Don't Know

Confession here.

I love to argue, create controversy, and get people all up in arms. I thrive on it.

I can be sitting at a family get-together, where everyone is actually getting along, and I will throw in some comment that I just know will spark some excitement.

"Do you do this on purpose?" my important Other asks, partly laughing, partly exasperated.

Yes, of course!

So this column was loads of fun for me.

I got to write stuff, that as I was writing, I know will land me some angry emails, phone calls, and outraged responses. And I was actually chuckling as I wrote because there is nothing I enjoy more than stirring up a hornet's nest. (I use calamine lotion for the stings that come my way. Very soothing.)

I had a funny feeling that this column would be one of those. And it was

Really, when one of the *Binah* editors asked me to write about this, I shot down the suggestion, feeling that I was not in the mood of being the target for everyone's darts. But then I remembered why I had originally begun writing about therapy — to educate people — and I remembered the me who is never afraid to say what I perceive as the truth or as right, and what made me go into this field to begin with: to help others, to be an advocate, to change the world (much easier than changing myself, and less time-consuming, so you will forgive me if I put my energies in the easier stuff!).

So here goes.

Deep breath, Mindy.

Topic sentence coming up.

Did you know that it is legal in New York State for minors — children under eighteen — to see a therapist without their parents' or guardians' permission?

Yup.

Exactly what you just heard.

It's true.

I know because I get calls about this all the time.

Teenagers call me because they feel desperate for therapy, but telling their parents is out of the question. For many reasons.

Principals of schools call me. Neighbors call me. They tell me, "We have a girl who needs therapy, but the parents cannot know. What should we do?"

Here is what I do first.

I ask, "Why can't the parents know about therapy?"

This question is important because I know that for the most part there is nobody as important in a child's life as his parents. Nobody loves that kid as much as his parents. And I believe very strongly that family is important. I believe that especially in our communities, where the family structure is so crucial, so strong, that parental involvement in — or at least knowledge of — their child's pain and attempts to heal, should be a given.

So I assess the situation to see if I can present an alternative to the secrecy. And usually I can.

But sometimes, when I cannot, I turn to New York State law that states the rights of a minor to enter therapy without her parents' knowledge.

I belong to the National Association for Social Workers (NASW), a national organization uniting those in the social work field. NASW was formed to create a place where social workers can gain knowledge about the issues that communities and the greater society face, form a more powerful forum for advocacy, provide continuing education, and receive a host of other services, among them legal advice.

When I was first faced with a question of treating a minor without parental consent, I contacted the Deputy General Counsel for NASW. The lawyer I spoke to informed me that while she cannot give me legal counsel, she can give me advice about legal issues relating to my field of practice.

In response to my query, she cited Section 22.11 from the NY Mental Hygiene that states a minor independently may seek treatment for drugs or alcohol. Section 33.21 cites that a minor can knowingly give consent for treatment when it is necessary for his or her well-being and there is no legal guardian reasonably available to provide consent.

The lawyer also informed me that if a minor can be considered competent enough to give consent for treatment, then that minor can also approve or reject the release of her confidential information to others (such as teachers, neighbors, or Rabbis).

So there you have it.

New York State is a great place to be a minor if you need therapy and it would be detrimental to the well-being of the minor if the parent(s) know about it.

It may be you are thinking that if one parent is not "reasonably available for consent," why not the other parent?

Good question.

I have found that often, when the child is afraid of a parent finding out he is going to therapy, or the parent refuses to allow therapy, then the child knows the other parent — who the child is not afraid of, and who may even want the child in therapy — cannot agree to something the other parent forbids. Often this is because the other parent is unable to stand up for the child in face of his or her spouse.

There are many questions that may come up. Can a parent who finds out later contest the legality of the minor's consent? Is there a minimum age at which a minor can give consent? If a parent finds out, can the parent revoke consent? What is even considered "reasonably unavailable" or "services necessary to a minor's well-being"?

These are valid questions, and ones which may scare therapists away from accepting minors into their practice; and I do not have all the answers. The wordings of these provisions are ambiguous and open to interpretation.

I wish children would not be suffering. I wish that when children suffer, their parents would be their advocates.

It is not an ideal situation to have a child come to therapy without parental consent. But when it is necessary, I am awed by the responsibility that principals, neighbors, relatives and Rabbanim take to protect a child and help her achieve the life she wants for herself.

And if I am called to be the therapist in that situation, I do what I need to do.

Eggs aimed at my head, anyone?

Therapy, Shmerapy

Just a Spoonful of Medicine Makes the Down Go Down...

Look, the only thing I can do is give you straight talk from the perspective of a therapist. I refuse to offer medical advice. I refuse to make the decision for you. I refuse to convince you one way or another whether or not to fill your prescription for Lexapro, Xanax, Wellbutrin, or Clonepine. I absolutely refuse. And here's why.

Little history lesson first.

It used to be that psychiatric wards were filled with lunatics. There were mental asylums jam-packed with "crazies." The conditions were awful and the prognosis even more so. Mental illness was nothing short of a death sentence, the chances of living a normal life virtually zero.

And then came the reforms. Do-gooders went into these places and demanded that people with mental illness be treated humanely. That definitely helped. Especially after one brave journalist wrote a powerful expose on life in one of these places.

So now the wards were cleaner, nicer, and the inmates treated more decently. But the people were still considered crazy; they still acted crazy.

Today, those places are mostly gone. No need for 'em anymore.

What happened to all those people?

They escaped.

How, you ask?

With the miraculous introduction of psychotropic drugs.

We live in a world where drugs can alleviate a variety of symptoms of mental illness so that once-crippling diagnoses now have optimistic prognoses.

People with bi-polar (originally called manic-depressive) disorder have the miracle drug lithium, which stabilizes them and allows them to lead functional lives in the comfort of mainstream society. The same goes for those with severe OCD, Tourette's Syndrome, and a host of other mental illnesses, which can be managed with a variety of psychotropic drugs.

Psychotropic drugs have almost single-handedly changed the way we view and live with mental illness.

History lesson over. Here's the essay question: What is the moral of the story? (I know, in history class you write essays about how history repeats itself, and morals are usually discussed in literature classes. Oh well, I'm the teacher here, so I can give whatever assignment I choose.)

The moral of the story? Sometimes you should definitely say yes to drugs.

Sometimes I get clients who are struggling so hard to improve their lives, fighting anxiety or depression, putting in Herculean efforts to change — and with a pill, the fight becomes easier, and life becomes more productive. I cheer on my clients who fight the good fight of mental illness with a combination of therapy and drugs.

But, but, but.

There's been an explosion of prescription drug usage by people who simply don't want to tolerate any feelings of discomfort.

Shidduchim is stressful? Suffering from insomnia? Complicated career choices? Take a pill.

Moving to a new house? Your daughter just had triplets? Pesach is coming up? Pop a pill.

Mother-in-law problems? Lost your job? Child refuses to be potty-trained? Swallow that pill.

I tell my clients, "Anxiety is a good thing. It's what motivates you to achieve. You just need to get that anxiety down to a level that it works *for* you, not *against* you."

Therapy, Shmerapy

When a new client comes into my office with anxiety and immediately asks about taking medication, I say, "Why don't you wait two or three sessions? Once you realize that your anxiety level can be decreased with therapy alone, you can make a more informed decision at that time."

I feel my role as a therapist is not only to help a client overcome the challenge that originally brought her to therapy, but to give her the tools to accept her anxiety as a strength and to learn how to manage it across *many* situations.

Using drugs to dull the anxiety robs a person of the chance to grow from the experience of that particular challenge because the entire challenge has been dulled.

When a person comes to therapy, even as an adjunct to taking drugs, at least he is working on the problem itself on some level. But many people avoid the anxious feelings, avoid the problems that provoke those anxious feelings, and avoid the messages behind the anxiety by reaching for the pill bottle.

Therapy is way harder than taking a pill. Way more time-consuming, painful, and challenging.

Pesach is stressful because your married daughter does not help? Yes, that pill will help you have a calmer Pesach because you simply won't care anymore. But the opportunity to teach your daughter and to develop a more honest and meaningful relationship with her has also been lost somewhere in that fuzzy calm.

With that pill, you are no longer stressed that you lost your job. Great! But you may have also lost the ability or motivation to figure out why you were fired and to make constructive changes that will improve your quality of life.

This new refusal to sit with our pain, to sit with our discomfort, to sit with our feelings that may not always be pleasant is also a refusal to grow as people.

A client suffering from anxiety walked into my office (Yes, she gave me permission to repeat this anecdote. Confidentiality, confidentiality, confidentiality!).

I explained to her how cognitive behavioral therapy (CBT) will work to alleviate her symptoms.

"Do I have to believe in this for it to work?" she asked me suspiciously, as if I was selling her some hocus pocus that required her to believe in fairies for the magic to manifest itself.

I laughed. "No," I said. "If you do the work, it's going to help even if you don't believe it will."

And it did.

Bring on the angry letters to the editor!

Therapy, Shmerapy

Form. Storm. Perform. Are you A Group Member Norm?

Here's how I walk into a crowd. A workshop, a wedding, a fundraiser.

I quickly scan the room. A quick study of the people flits through my head. Who do I know here? What type of crowd is this?

Then I decide where to sit. The seat itself would be best near an entrance. A door. A window.

I would rather sit alone than make small talk. I like to think. To listen to the music at the wedding or take notes at the workshop. I can easily sit alone at a table and feel perfectly content, even annoyed, if someone projects her own insecurities on me, decides to feel bad for me and joins me.

When I join a group, around a table at a wedding, in a class, or on a random bus trip, I am quiet at first. I don't know if I want to expend energy talking to people in whom I may realize I have no interest. But I do not want to be rude, so I smile, answer questions, and generally behave myself. I am not, however, forthcoming.

But very soon, as I get warmed up, I become opinionated, funny, and allow myself to become vulnerable, to allow myself to be known by the others.

I go through many stages in a group. And when I am in a group long enough, who I am outside of the group is played out in technicolor right there within the group dynamics. Even if I meet with my group only once a month, after a year, my group will have a good idea of how I behave at work, at home, and with others with whom I have close contact even on a daily basis. Because a group becomes a social microcosm. The group setting becomes the same interpersonal universe a person inhabits outside of the parameters of the group.

Every person who joins a group, willingly or unwillingly, consciously or subconsciously, reveals the most innermost part of themselves when they hang out there long enough.

And even as I know this, I cannot camouflage myself, I cannot pretend, I cannot protect myself from exposing my weaknesses, even demonstrating my strengths, when I am in my writing group, my various therapy supervision groups, sitting in a circle at the bungalow colony.

Which is why group therapy is one of the most powerful therapeutic tools, though very underutilized in the religious community.

As a therapist, when I sit with my clients, I only know them from what they tell me. From their body language, from their tears, and from the issues they grapple with. And that's fine. Therapy works, regardless. But I also know that most clients come to therapy because of a desire to improve relationships in their lives. They say they want to find a job and point to their lack of organization, skills or ability to commit to time as their presenting issue; but as we go deeper into therapy, what becomes clearer is that their distorted sense of self, their inability to connect to others, feelings of inferiority in relation to others is what is truly inhibiting their chances of gainful employment.

Individual therapy works. As a relational therapist, I am always assessing the here-and-now experience of the therapeutic relationship because it gives me insight into what the client is experiencing outside of therapy if I can see it played out within the therapy hour.

If a client is late (I know — such a trite example!), I am already wondering. Is this a chronic issue? How does that affect her out-of-therapy commitments? Relationships? What does her lateness mean? As her therapist, though, I must be careful to align myself with her because as long as she is coming to therapy, even though she is late to each session, her arrival is also telling me something. So I may not address her lateness necessarily, because the client comes to discuss other things, and I am respectful and mindful to be *where the client is*. But I wonder about that lateness and when we will finally get to talk about it.

In a group, the process is accelerated. Other group members, not bound by a therapist's limitations, can confront the tardy member immediately. Demand compliance with the group rules of being on time. Force the client to explain her frequent lateness. Give suggestions to be on time.

What can take many months in individual therapy can unfold much quicker within a group.

It can take months for a client to display anger towards me. Or reveal how she manages hurt, upset, disappointment, shame. But in a group, the dynamics of the other members force these social interactions much quicker. The group allows the therapist leading the group to notice and facilitate when the other members begin to react so as to allow for corrective emotional experiences in a safe environment.

There are stages of group dynamics. My favorite rendition of group dynamics is a simple one coined by psychologist Bruce Tucker. Forming. Storming. Norming. Performing. And sometimes also Adjourning/ Mourning.

Although there are different types of groups, these stages would apply to many of them. Notice them in your classroom when you put girls into groups or assign jobs for yearbook. In camp performances where a cast must work together. In a class or bunk in and of itself. Sisters-in-law in a family, especially as the group expands and changes with new members. In ongoing supervision groups, in interactive workshop modules like parenting groups.

In the *forming stage*, everyone is polite. Maybe excited. Nervous. Roles are not always clear. Rules are established.

In the *storming stage*, personalities begin to emerge as individuals push against set boundaries. When personalities or working/learning styles clash, dyadic alignments occur, problems crop up and roles begin to evolve or be assigned. The leader. The organizer. The mother. The peacemaker. Some negative roles begin to evolve as well. The complainer. The shirker. The martyr. The drama queen. The silent. The monopolist. And still other roles, like the comedian. The information-provider. The note-taker. The blocker.

In the *norming stage*, differences begin to be resolved, strengths of individuals and the group begins to emerge, and the group starts to form into a cohesive unit as positive feelings towards other group members develop. The task of the group is addressed in this stage.

As the group enters the *performing stage*, the task of the group is addressed at its deepest and most functional level. The structures and supports that have been set up are working. The group feels like a team and is committed to its goals.

Lastly, when the group is *adjourning*, as many groups must, there is a *mourning* process. It's time to say goodbye after the project is done, the performance is over, the parenting series has ended. It's how the individuals say their goodbyes, readjust without the group, and perhaps evolve after disbandment into new types of relationships, continued growth, or simply moving on.

Even if you are not a therapist, being aware of these dynamics as a teacher, principal of a new school, bunk counselor, workshop leader, or even mother-in-law welcoming a new child into the family, can improve your ability to enhance relationships. To facilitate the inevitable stages. To address the relationship component. To get the job done.

If you want to sit next to me at a workshop, you can join me near the door. And maybe the forming stage will eventually lead to the performing stage in which we can work well together.

Therapy, Shmerapy

EMDR Is More Than Just Some Random Letters in the Alphabet Soup of Fancy Initials

I did it.

"Did what?" you want to know.

Did a two-week training program to learn EMDR.

Okay, okay. I see you rolling your eyes. A bunch of new letters these mental health professionals came up with.

Hey, EMDR is much easier to say (and spell) than Eye Movement Desensitization Reprocessing (not that it makes any more sense when you spell it out).

But let me tell you, this training blew my mind. I think it was the very first time that I attended a training seminar that not only did I find fascinating (because I have also found psychodrama and equestrian therapy fascinating), but also immediately relevant and applicable.

EMDR was developed by Francine Shapiro almost accidentally when she was walking in the park and noticed that, when she had disturbing thoughts, her eye movements caused the disturbing thoughts to lose their charge, to lose their intensity, until they no longer bothered her.

She went ahead and created a whole therapy based on this interplay of disturbing thoughts and eye movements that has helped thousands of people overcome traumas, phobias and whatnot.

It sounds ridiculous, I know. It sounds too ludicrously easy to work, I know.

But it does.

EMDR has been researched extensively, and the research has

consistently shown its efficacy.

During Hurricane Katrina, first responders used EMDR on survivors. In my professional peer group of elite practitioners from all over the country who work primarily with severe trauma, after initials like PsyD, LMH, LCSW, and MD, inevitably EMDR follows. They are all trained in it.

It is not a passing phase; it is here to stay, and I am so glad I learned it.

Lots of people have heard of the initials, but much fewer know what they stand for or what EMDR is. Here goes:

EMDR is therapy that although it has many of the components of standard therapy like obtaining a client history and stabilizing a client in crisis, its theoretical underpinnings are based on how trauma organizes itself in the brain and impacts a person's functioning. According to EMDR, when a trauma happens, the incident remains frozen in the brain. In the same way that something frozen can stay in that same state indefinitely, so too that traumatic memory can stay frozen together with all the sights, smells, feelings and thoughts that accompanied the original traumatic incident.

And here's the problem. After that trauma, anytime something touches upon that frozen memory, it activates the same feelings, thoughts, and even smells or visions that were frozen along with the memory, even if those feelings don't make sense in the new context.

Say you were six years old when you were in the Purim play in first grade and once onstage, you started crying from stage fright.

It may be a funny story retold years later, but if that incident was traumatic for you, the image of being onstage, the smells of the glue and glitter, and the feeling of being in the bright light may have been stored in your brain and frozen. And now, Elmer's glue makes you nauseous. You sweat each time you need to make a phone call to your daughter's teacher. Or taking pictures by your son's bar mitzvah makes you squirm.

An EMDR therapist, after the standard history taking and assessment phase, will ask which problem brings the client to therapy, and will then

Therapy, Shmerapy

access the client's memories that cluster around that presenting problem. A presenting problem can be fear of starting a job, going on a date, or a troubled relationship with a friend, spouse, or child.

For the client who started crying from stage fright, memories may include other plays in elementary school, eighth grade graduation, a tenth grade speech, or refusing to recite the *Ma Nishtanah* at the Pesach *seder*.

The therapist would help the client access the negative, self-referencing belief(s) she holds about herself when thinking of the memory. A negative belief frozen in time, such as when she cried at the Purim play, may be something like: *I am a disappointment* or *I am inadequate* or *I am a failure*.

EMDR would target the *earliest* or *worst* memory, and then begin the process called *desensitization*. And here's the part that seems really, really strange.

Sitting across from the client, the therapist will use her fingers in a sweeping motion back and forth in front of the client's eyes and ask the client to bring up the image associated with the negative memory, think of his negative belief associated with the chosen memory, and advise him to be aware of any associated physical sensations noted in his body. The bilateral stimulation of the eyes in conjunction with the thoughts serves to unfreeze the memory and work through it so that the memory remains but without the associated disturbances, without the associated negative beliefs or triggers.

Some therapists, instead of eye movement, offer bilateral stimulation with *tappers*, in which a person feels bilateral movements in her left and right hands alternatively. Others use light or sounds. But the premise remains the same.

Not all clients are good candidates for EMDR.

A inappropriate candidate for this therapy is a client who is unable to self-soothe. Or cannot verbalize (there is EMDR for children that works slightly differently).

I will tell you a secret. I tried EMDR. At the workshop. We had to practice on each other. And when a colleague practiced on me, I was supposed to think of a memory to use. So, I'm not crazy, you know. I am not doing therapy with this person I barely know, using some strange method she just learned two hours earlier. So I choose a real simple memory. No charge to it. Couldn't care less about this memory to begin with. Bah! No sweat letting her do her funny fingers stuff on me.

But the joke was on me. And the joke was on my colleague who changed places, giving me a turn to be her EMDR therapist and choosing a memory *she* thought was benign.

It blew us both away.

I cleared a memory, a negative belief, and some associated painful feelings while allowing her to do the EMDR on me. And the same happened to her.

So that's it.

I'm sold on it.

EMDR, anybody? It's great stuff...

Therapy, Shmerapy

Sandtray Therapy

A few years ago, I walked into a colleague's therapy office, and I didn't want to leave. From floor to ceiling, her shelves were lined with hundreds of miniatures. Miniature people, objects, and landscapes; realistic, fantastical, magical, and mythical. And in the center of her room was a sandbox.

"Sandtray therapy," she said, noticing my reaction. "I do sandtray with my clients."

Her clients were adults, not children.

When I was a student of social work interning in an agency, I worked with children. The method of therapy was play therapy. I remember walking into a play therapy room for the first time, and all I wanted to do was get onto the floor and play with the Lego and dolls and dollhouse and the modeling clay. Most of all, I itched to dig my hands into the clay and simply create, to feel the sensation of the clay in my hands. And when my little clients played with clay, I picked up the clay and played with them.

I don't work with children anymore. But the awe of play therapy and the magic of sandtray therapy inspired me. And when I finally found a training workshop in sandplay therapy, I registered and created an area in my therapy office in which clients could use the sand as another tool of therapy. Often, when I am finished work for the day, I uncover my sandbox, a 12" X 19½" box that stands on a rolling cart, randomly choose miniatures from my shelves, and play. I do not think about what I do. I just choose my miniatures and then place them in the sand, creating a sandtray. When I finish, I take a step back and watch what I have done.

I do not take pictures because it would be as revealing as leaving my personal diary around. I learn a lot about myself in that time.

What is sandtray therapy?

Sandtray therapy is the use of miniatures and sand. It is a kinesthetic experience, the sheer pleasure of running one's hands through the sand, of handling the miniatures, that often allows for the release of verbal communication.

Actually, there are two terms used for the use of sand and miniatures in therapy: sandtray and sandplay. Sandtray refers to an eclectic usage of this therapy, relying on many modalities of therapy, while sandplay refers specifically to a Jungian theory in therapy (if you care to know more, you can look it up). There are specifications as to how large the sand tray needs to be, requirements that it be a blue sand tray; the categories of miniatures with which to begin a collection for use in therapy (people, structures, plants, animals, vehicles, and magical objects — to name a few), criteria for the depth of the sand in the tray, and an allowance for the use of both wet and dry sand.

Then there's the symbolism of various objects. Candles symbolize hope and transformation; snakes are a threat. Objects and people may be buried under the sand; flooded sand represents a lack of boundaries.

Sandtray is not conventional therapy, but neither is it unconventional. It is used as an adjunct to either play with children, or to connect with adults as a non-verbal tool. It is another way to talk — or motivate talk. It is useful to the client as simply another medium to alleviate the distress or symptoms that brings a client into therapy. And the same way therapists can come from various orientations (Gestalt, Jungian, object relations, psychoanalytic...) and yet use "talk" in session; so too therapists can use sand and remain true to their orientation, using the symbolism of the sand and its other elements to "talk."

Take, for example, a client who creates a sandtray in which she dumps a variety of animals into the sand. Then she places one oversized tiger in the center and stuffs a little penguin under the sand, removed from view.

Therapy, Shmerapy

In this symbolic representation, she is showing the therapist — and then may verbalize as well — how she is the penguin buried under the chaos at home, fearful of an older sister who bullies her, or how she feels unheard. The actual sand and tray and miniatures have their own meaning and methods and techniques as any other modality has, like CBT and EMDR, or even the traditional talk therapy.

I have a client (who has graciously allowed me to share this anecdote with you) who cannot speak because of the pain she carries. She is a beautiful human being, sensitive, caring, talented, and deep.

When she saw the new shelves of miniatures, she was overwhelmed. She did not want to look at them, to touch them. It was as if the words she had buried inside of her, the stories she would not remember, were sitting on the shelves in plain sight. She refused to engage in sandtray even though I thought (what do I know, right?) it would be a way to help her speak, even without words.

But we talked about sandtray therapy in an abstract way. Not about her. In general. Sometimes we do that. Talk generally. Because the specifics are too painful. And because she is intelligent. And because she works with children, so any kind of play medium piques her interest. And I tell her about my sandtray training experience.

At the training, our instructor showed us slides of one client's sandtrays over a course of time. The beginning ones were chaotic, the symbolism raw. Wrecked parties. People sprawled on the floor, the table overturned and the little objects scattered in and about the sand. Later sandtrays showed some people upright, the birthday table a little less messy. And the themes of the sandtray continued to emerge in different images the client created.

And then another picture of the sandtray flashed across the screen, and there was a collective gasp from our group. The sandtray was a simply marvelous; one could not help but gasp at its beauty.

"There is," our instructor explained, "a geometric pattern that occurs in nature that has a definite center. In sandtray a client will create it spontaneously at a time when they are experiencing a centeredness, a grounding, when therapy is healing." Pointing to the screen, the instructor said, "In the four corners of the sandtray, the client put protective objects or figures. This is another aspect of this geometric pattern that occurs spontaneously."

My client left after the session, and the next morning I received a text from her. "After our session yesterday, I thought I would share what my [four-year-old] daughter drew this morning. She happens to be in a good place currently."

Attached to the text was a remarkable drawing by this child. A geometric pattern, the perfect symmetry of four corners boldly delineated, and a definite center.

There is the most beautiful concept in sandtray play of the *liminal*. *Liminal* refers to that space **in-between** that is prevalent in the cycles of life, seasons, and day. The liminal time of day and night is twilight — the space that is neither day nor night. In that space, change can occur.

The liminal space between land and water is the beach; the sand.

And with sandtray therapy, we give the client that liminal space in the therapy room; their very own beach, their very own sand, where change can occur.

Therapy, Shmerapy

The One I Don't Speak About

I am an attachment therapist. I view my clients' problems through a lens of attachment theory — that we how we are nurtured as infants and children, how we form relationships with our primary caregivers is how we learn to relate to our world as adults.

A reader writes, *"I read your column about the woman who wanted a hug from her therapist. I was shocked because I feel the same way. I know I have had a very bad relationship with my mother and I sometimes feel like I wish my therapist was my mother. At other times, I am so furious at my therapist. My feelings are very confusing because they range from anger to love and back again. Sometimes I miss her so much in between sessions that it hurts; sometimes I just want to skip a session. I don't even know how to talk to her about all of this. Why am I feeling like this? What can I do about it?"*

The above reader is experiencing *transference* with her therapist. The transference is the phenomenon of how clients transfer feelings from past relationships onto the therapist.

Although I may use other interventions borrowed from different theories, through the lens of attachment I watch for the transference that is bound to occur. How I become that mother figure in the therapy room. The wishing for closeness and love; the fury and hurt of rejection.

There is a duality in therapy. The *content* of the session and the *context*. We may be talking about the difficulties dealing with a boss (content) but the context, the meaning of the session, is really about relationship difficulties stemming from childhood when the mother was boss.

And there comes the duality of the therapeutic relationship; firstly, two people working together for a client's benefit and secondly, the superimposed transference in which the therapist-as-person almost ceases to exist and is instead replaced by the *object* of the transference. Often the mother.

As an object relations therapist I heed not only the context of the session material but also the transference.

And from that point the work of therapy evolves, in which a person is reborn in the therapy room, self-actualizing to become all he or she can be.

Here is The Transference — the unspoken dialogue occurring between you and your therapist. The dance between the attachment therapist and her client. It is the context of any session, no matter what you speak about.

The client: The one I don't speak about is my therapist. There is nothing to speak about. Not how her room wraps me up and holds me tight. Or how I can lay down my burden, the anxiety that chokes me, and melt into the room's warmth. What do I tell my family and friends who hover around me, watching me worriedly, their presence suffocating? That I count the minutes until I am enveloped securely in her room, leaving the world outside its walls, that she has become the most important person in my life?

The therapist: The one you don't speak about is your mother.

The client: I do not speak about my therapist because there is no one who would understand. She listens without judgment as I speak about terrible things I have done. I watch her as I speak, for any sign of disapproval, but she is listening, and I know she is so present for me, that nothing and nobody else exists for her in that moment, as no one else exists for me. Even in my fury at her, her room is my sanctuary.

Therapy, Shmerapy

The therapist: The one you don't speak of is your mother. When you were just an infant, in the symbiotic relationship where there was no *other*, just one continuous being and you could not differentiate where you ended and she began; when she was the source of food and comfort and pleasure, the all-encompassing being that was the foundation of all you needed and wanted, where did the cracks begin? When did you begin to feel she could not provide you with what you needed, creating a void of hunger that feels insatiable even today so many years later?

The client: There is nothing to say about my therapist because it shames me to love someone so much. Her laugh, and the way her eyes seem bottomless from behind her solemn glasses, all make me want to create a reaction in her. To make her care for me as I care for her. I want to know her as she knows me. I am afraid of loving so intensely. I cannot talk about the fear that I am essentially unlovable.

The therapist: If you would speak of your mother, we would unravel the threads that have bound you so tightly into this anxious knot of fear and shame. As you moved away from the symbiotic relationship of the newborn, and began to realize to realize your *otherness*, that you are an entity apart from her, why did you not realize her love for you, that as separate as she is from you, you are still her child? Was she unresponsive to your cries, preoccupied with her own life of bills or illness or worries or struggles that took her away from you, as you watched her from between the bars of crib, feeling helplessly alone?

The client: My therapist is the pacifier that plugs a hole inside of me. I do not speak of how I talk to her imaginary presence and tell her how I am angry at her, or about the things I want to accomplish in my life, or spill out the hurt that she will not take me home with her so I can be her child. I know she cares about me; I hear it in her silence and in the questions she asks. One time, when I spoke about — when I spoke about — when I spoke about that time, I can almost swear there were tears in her eyes. I can read her body language and facial expressions, feel her around me even when I turn my face away as I talk, avert my eyes to hide myself from her. I know she will always find me.

The therapist: Why won't you speak of your mother? When you were two years old, were you able to immerse yourself in the pleasures of your neighbor's foreign living room, secure in the knowledge of your mother's presence, or was your playtime punctuated by bursts of anxiety that she would disappear at any minute, abandoning you? Was your attachment avoidant, clingy, or secure?

When you brought home from school your arts and crafts, when you smiled at her, when you gave her gifts of your day, did she mirror your delight in being your mother, or did she reprimand you for being the child you were? In her presence did you feel safe that you were cherished and adored, or did you experience the anxiety that has since dogged your nights, the butterflies that have taken residence in your stomach each morning?

The client: My therapist talks about the *transference*. She angers me. This has nothing to do with my mother. This is about my therapist. How I love her. How I struggle to feel her love and caring for me. How I rage at her, how I want to bring down the stars as a gift for her, how my world has been condensed into the hour a week I see her. I wish she was my mother. If she would be, I could be happy. Confident. Successful. Thin. Have friends. A job. I could be or do anything if my therapist would be my mother. If she would tell me how good I am. How wonderful I am. Know me and my desires and fears and worries and successes. My therapist is a warm bath each week. I splash in her waters, but when I leave her office, I am afraid that the waters of her life close up, leaving no sign that I have been there. I speak *to* her; I do not speak of *her*.

The therapist: The one you do not speak of is your mother. In therapy, you feel the drenching rage of the transference. "Be my mother!" you demand, and when I cannot fill that void, your fury erupts, the hot lava cascading into pools on the carpeted floor, the room blazing up from the roiling ground, bombs exploding and shattering the walls as glass emotions break and flame. Finally, smoke, the remnants of your rage, blankets the room, snuffing out the fire of fury and the session is over.

The client: (*sigh*) If you promise to hold me here in your heart, I will speak.

PART V THE THERAPY

Living With a Therapist

"Why don't you write about what it's like to live with a therapist,'" my husband suggests.

"I don't want to make my readers jealous that they don't have an in-house therapist," I say.

"If *I* write the column," my husband counters, "they will know that they have nothing to be jealous of."

So this column is for all those married to therapists who wish their spouses had normal jobs, for all those whose parents are therapists and wish that therapists' kids were not known for being nuts, and for all the rest of my readers who sometimes wish a therapist lived in their house.

I am part of a professional group of therapists comprised of psychiatrists, social workers, psychologists, and PhDs. We are talking about highly educated people, many who, aside from the work they do in the field of mental health, also write prestigious books and articles in peer-reviewed journals, are professors in universities, spearhead projects, research studies, and workshops; and are innovators and leaders in their fields. (And then there is me!)

So I send a message to the group.

"I am writing a column and would like feedback about the struggles you hear from your spouses and children who face the daily challenge of living with a therapist in the house."

Whew.

Must have hit a real hot topic because in a short time, the responses came in thick and fast.

• • •

Therapy, Shmerapy

"My wife's complaint during a discussion or argument [is] 'Would you say that to one of your clients?' to which I respond, 'That is why you are my wife and not a client.'"

"My daughter says she's going to start a [support] group for children of therapists."

"Aside from the immersion required by me to understand and treat complex trauma and dissociation every day, the main complaint I get from my wife is that no matter what my relationship skills might be in the therapy room, they don't have relevance at home. In other words, I get zero points for any clinical acumen I might demonstrate."

"One day, when my son was about fourteen and we had one of our you-just-don't-understand moments, he looked at me and shook his head with an expression somewhere between pity and patronizing on his face and said, 'It's so hard to believe you're a therapist!' Ouch!"

"[It's taboo to share my] interpretation within the household...[I may] NEVER pathologize [family members]."

"... My tween often asks where she can find a therapist like her mom, and my husband reminds me that 'I am not one of your patients...' I love what I do and would do it for free. I have to remind myself that [being a] a therapist is only a part of who I am."

"What problem? I'm a THERAPIST. I [am supposed to] know all, understand all, and [can] never [be] wrong. My twenty-three-year-old son recently said to me, 'I am shocked [today at] what came out of your therapist mouth.'"

"My ten-year-old daughter [calls] me a nooooroosiiichoooologist as if I have some disease she hopes never to catch. I don't know when I completed the irreversible metamorphose into therapist, but I do know some individuals (and I am not pointing fingers!) who have something to say about it."

• • •

I remember when my children were young, they begged me to just yell. "You talk very quietly," they accused me. "It's better if you just give a good smack or scream. Your quiet talking is much scarier."

"I'm not interested in you *listening* when I talk to you," my husband says. "I don't want you *empathizing* with me. You are supposed to argue with me. You are not supposed to *validate* me. You need to try and convince me that *you* are right!"

Members of my group describe other experiences.

• • •

"I find I have lost some of my spontaneous emotional response and sympathy with family because of my training and experience with empathy and [containment]."

"In my early days as a clinician I found myself stuck in therapist mode even at home, which was not appreciated. Nowadays, if my husband and I are arguing, he'll say, 'Would you please talk to me like one of your clients? Where did all the empathy go?'"

• • •

So let me create a synopsis of what it's like to live with a therapist.

A parent or spouse who also happens to be a therapist is never supposed to act like a therapist. No interpretations of why a person may be acting obnoxious or angry; absolutely no diagnosis of behaviors. No listening, validating, or empathizing. No using a quiet therapist voice. No modeling of appropriate relational skills. No empowering of others to figure out their own solutions to problems.

Fair enough.

But heaven forbid, if a mother-therapist acts like a mother — you know, doing motherly things such as telling everyone else how to get the job done or how to act normal, getting frustrated when they don't, raising her voice above a whisper, saying the wrong thing, not getting it or totally missing the point —everyone *else* is allowed to say, "And *you* are supposed to be the therapist around here."

I asked my kids the same question I asked my therapist-group.

"You act like a therapist all the time," one son informed me. "You see everything through the eyes of a therapist." He thought for a moment.

"Everyone does that, really," he said. "I also look at things through my own lens [as a yeshivah boy]. So maybe it's not a problem. Just different."

Maybe that's why this response seemed so familiar: "I'm not sure if it's because he is a psychologist or just an exemplary father, but many moons ago when our daughter was fifteen... [she] threw herself on the sofa crying, 'You're so reasonable, you make it impossible for me to hate you!'"

The last response I received from my group at the end of the day (and right before I finished this column) summed up this conundrum of parent-spouse-therapist perfectly.

"Being a child of [two therapists] and having ended up in the field myself, [I am reminded] of how my dad used to ask me how I'd *feel* about washing the car. My response? 'Not too good, Dad,' was worth the try, but in the end I had to do it to get my allowance, so the parent in him eventually won."

I am going to start a support group for therapists who face the daily challenge of living with spouses and children.

Goodbye —
A Client Terminates

Therapist, teacher, sister, savior
Summers have returned because of you;
Colleague, friend, mentor, mother,
Therapist, I thank you.
For the dark wintry days
Your warmth and wisdom thawed;
For healing the child inside
I had always thought was flawed;
For your mothering presence
That calmed a raging storm;
For the tears and laughter shared
That carried me back from harm.
In everything you do, you're not just a therapist;
But mother, mentor, sister, and friend too,
Rolled up in one;
There's no one else quite like you.
If I could wrap up my love in a hug in a box,
I would send it to you.

GLOSSARY

frum	adj. religious, referring to a Jew
apikorsus	n. heresy
aveilus	n. period of mourning according to Jewish tradition
avodas Hashem	n. G-dly work, referring to a Jew's striving to become a better person
b'show	n. date, referring to the chassidic custom of dating by setting up a meeting between a potential bride and groom in the home
bas mitzvah	n. Yiddish reference to the passage of rites of a Jewish girl turning 12 who assumes responsibility for keeping the laws according to the Torah (compared to the bar mitzvah for when a boy turns 13; also bat mitzvah)
chametz	n. leavened foods forbidden on Passover
chas v'shalom	interj. Hebrew phrase meaning G-d forbid. Literally translated as "completely disgraced"
chassan	n. groom
chavrusa	n. Torah learning partner
chessed	n. charitable acts
emunah	n. faith
gabbai	n. originally Aramaic word meaning tax collector; referring today to a synagogue official with administrative duties
Hakodosh Boruch Hu	n. G-d; lit. Hebrew "Holy One, Blessed Be He"

halachah	n. body of Jewish law and tradition comprising the laws of the Bible; here, referring to specific rulings of Jewish law
halachic	adj. referring to halachah
Hashem	n. G-d ;lit. the Name
hashkafos	n. ideological outlook from a Torah perspective
kallah	n. bride
kibud av v'em	n. the act of honoring one's father and mother
Klal Yisroel	n. the Jewish People
Kohen	n. member of the Jewish priestly class, descending from the tribe of Levi; here referring to halachic status
kollel	n. institute for full-time Torah study
Ma Nishtana	n. the Four Questions asked at the Passover Seder
mashpi'im	n. pl. spiritual mentors
mechanech	n. teacher
menahel	n. principal
menaheles	fem. menahel
mentsch	n. person of integrity, honor and noble character; lit. Yiddish "human being"
mentschen	pl. mentsch
mitzvos	n. pl. good deeds
mussar sefarim	n. pl. books teaching ethics
nisayon	n. test
p'sak	n. halachic ruling
Pesach	n. Passover holiday
rabbanim	pl. rabbis
Rav	n. rabbi
Rebbetzin	n. rabbi's wife
redt	v. to speak
redts	v. pl. redt
Rosh Yeshivah	n. scholar, head of a yeshivah

seder	n. the unit of time allotted for learning in a yeshiva setting
Shabbos	n. Shabbat
Shabbosim	pl. Shabbos
she'eilah	n. halachic question
shaliach	n. messenger
shalom bayis	n. marital harmony; lit. Hebrew "peace in the home"
shidduch	n. match for marriage
shiur	n. lecture
shlemazel	n. unlucky person
shloshim	n. 30 days of mourning according to Jewish Law
sho'el eitzah	v. ask a halachic question
shochet	n. ritual slaughterer
shul	n. synagogue
simcha	n. celebration
simchos	pl. simcha(h)
tafkid	n. purpose
Tehillim	n. Psalms
teshuvah	n. repentance
treif	adj. not kosher
Totty	Daddy
yelados yekaros	interj. Hebrew term of endearment meaning "precious girls"
yeshivah	n. place of study
Yiddishkeit	n. Judaism
Yosef HaTzaddik	n. Joseph the Righteous

About the Author

Mindy Blumenfeld, LCSW, knows herself (duh, she is a therapist) but because other people may not, her editors recommended inserting this little bio into her book.

Mindy maintains a private practice in Brooklyn, New York, treating teens and adults. Mindy is a popular columnist for Binah Magazine and gives workshops and lectures at various events.

She loves reading, 'riting, and rollerblading (the 3 'Rs' of any proper education), and hugging grandchildren (specifically hers, but she's been spotted hugging others', too).

For speaking engagements – or just to let her know how much you loved her book (even if you just borrowed it from your neighbor) – she can be contacted at mindy.blumenfeld@gmail.com.

Look her up on LinkedIn:
   https://www.linkedin.com/in/mindy-blumenfeld-a8067583
Visit her blog at:
   https://nefeshinternational. org/blogs/MindyBlumenfeldLCSW